Praying 15 Days with

PETER JULIAN EYMARD

THE "PRAYING 15 DAYS" COLLECTION

SOURCE BOOKS

- To spend 15 days in the company of a spiritual master, similar to retreat days which break through our daily routine.

PRACTICAL BOOKS

- A biographical sketch at the beginning of the book
- A summary of the journey at the outset
- A help to prayer presented in each of the 15 chapters
- A detailed bibliography for further reading

EASY ACCESSIBILITY

- A resource for busy Christians which goes directly to core values
- Key information provided for the general public.

Praying 15 Days with

PETER JULIAN EYMARD

The Saint of the Eucharist

By Manuel Barbiero

Nouvelle Cité

PETER JULIAN EYMARD, THE EUCHARIST: THE PASSION OF HIS LIFE (1811-1868)

God led St. Peter Julian Eymard through a unique life journey to become the founder of two religious congregations, the Religious of the Blessed Sacrament and the Servants of the Blessed Sacrament, to plan an association for the laity inspired with the same charism, to envision an association for the spiritual and Eucharistic formation of the secular clergy, and to provide the inspiration for International Eucharistic Congresses. Pope John Paul II presented him to the whole Church as an "eminent apostle of the Eucharist" (December 9th 1995).

Peter Julian Eymard's life was marked by several stages. After a stay with the Oblates of

Mary Immaculate in Marseilles (1829) he entered the Major Seminary of Grenoble (1831). He was ordained as a priest (1834), and named as parochial vicar at Chatte (1834-1837), then later as pastor for the parish of Monteynard (1837-1839). Pursuing his call to religious life, he entered the Marists (1839) where he remained until the foundation of the Congregation of the Blessed Sacrament in Paris (May 13, 1856). All these passages give us a glimpse of an interior journey which was Eymard's.

The Eymard family had emigrated to La Mure d'Isère in search of work (1804) and had settled there. Family life was austere, marked by suffering, yet simultaneously fervent and welcoming. Julian Eymard, the father of Peter Julian, had married twice. He had grieved for two wives and eight of his ten children. He had welcomed an adopted daughter into his family. He opposed Peter Julian categorically when the latter expressed his desire to become a priest. It was at the shrine of Our Lady of Laus that Peter Julian would go to find the consolation which enabled him to maintain his decision. He studied Latin secretly to prepare himself for the seminary while engaged at the family workshop.

He practiced his ministry in the diocese of Grenoble during a five year period. He dedicated himself fully to his pastoral ministry giving special attention to the poor and the sick. He was aware of his limited and fragmented intellectual formation, and so he would continue his personal formation throughout his life. He was open to new fields of information, sustained by the Word of God, the Fathers of the Church, and the doctrine of the council of Trent.

During his ministry at Chatte (1834-1837) he received a grace which liberated him from a negative view of God, and obtained a positive view centered on God's love. His attraction to religious life led him to seek the permission of his bishop to leave the diocese and enter the Marists.

Father Eymard began his novitiate in Lyons on August 20, 1839. During the month of November 1839, he was assigned as spiritual director at the high school seminary of Belley by Father Jean-Claude Colin, the superior general. There, he made his profession of vows on February 16, 1840. His ministry with the children and the youth was very fruitful.

Beginning in November 1844, Father Colin called him to Lyons as Assistant General and, in 1846, designated him as Visitor General. In December 1845 Father Colin entrusted him with the direction of the Third Order of Mary. Father Eymard applied himself to develop this lay branch of Marists which he diversified into several groups, according to the different states of life. He provided its structure and set down its basic rules.

Peter Julian came to a better understanding of his vocation under the impulse of deep yet simple graces.

During the procession of the Blessed Sacrament from the church of St. Paul in Lyons on the Feast of Corpus Christi in 1845, he was struck with such a strong feeling of faith in Jesus Christ and Jesus Christ Eucharistic that he asked God for a grace of apostolic zeal like that of St. Paul.

His stay in Lyons brought him many enriching relationships. Father Eymard came to know the Curé d'Ars, Pauline Jaricot, Colin, Champagnat, Antoine Chevrier, etc. He became acquainted with the foreign missions, workers' circles and intellectual world (the mystical school of Lyons) as well.

While he was provincial, he visited the Marist house in Paris in 1849. There, he discovered the movement for nocturnal Adoration and at the same time, met Count Raymond de Cuers who would become his first companion in the Eucharistic foundation. He also met the foundress of Adoration Réparatrice, Mother Marie-Thérèse Dubouché.

On January 21, 1851, at the Shrine of Notre Dame

de Fourvière (Lyons), he discerned the urgency of working for the renewal of christian life by means of the Eucharist and he grasped the importance of a deeper formation for priests and laity.

Father Eymard felt a growing attraction toward the sacrament of the Eucharist, which he saw as a great grace chosen by God to restore faith and love in the modern world.

In fact, the world around him was in the midst of profound changes. The basis for a secular society, free of the Church's influence, had been laid by the Revolution and Napoleon.

The steam engine was the news of the day, coal and iron mines were swallowing up thousands of human beings; industrialization was taking over and submitting human beings to its own rhythm. The exodus from countryside to city had begun.

The first achievements of this new technology had begun to surface: railroads, photography, telegraph, medicine, navigation, etc. The middle class placed its faith only in progress and the future of science; it was also anti-clerical. A working class was born, destined to remain without rights for quite some time.

At La Seyne-sur-Mer, Father Eymard experienced a new calling on April 18, 1853. It was a "grace of self-donation," in view of the eucharistic projects which he was developing with Raymond de De Cuers and a few others. This new call led him to make the sacrifice of leaving the Marist congregation in order to found the Congregation of the Blessed Sacrament.

Finally, amidst many difficulties, his project was accepted on May 13, 1856 by the Archbishop of Paris, Mgr. Sibour. The Eucharistic life which Peter Julian proposed would not limit itself solely to the contemplative dimension; he wanted to embrace the Eucharistic thought as a whole, to join together both the active and contemplative aspects, to adore and lead others to adoration, to work for the first communion of young workers; he wanted to set fire to the four corners of France. "*A purely contemplative life*, he wrote, *cannot be fully Eucharistic; the hearth has a flame*. (CO 1030-CO 1032*)

On January 6, 1857, he inaugurated the first community of adorers with exposition of the Blessed Sacrament; the Society had four members at that time. Life was organized in conditions of poverty and destitution. Then, the community developed gradually.

Marguerite Guillot arrived in Paris from Lyons on May 25, 1858, and on the following July 2, Father Eymard named her to head the little group of candidates who had come to Paris for the foundation of the feminine branch, the Servants of the blessed Sacrament.

From the start, and throughout his ministry, Father Eymard's apostolate was multiform. He associated the laity to his undertaking through the Aggregation of the Blessed Sacrament; he organized the First communion for Adults for young workers, rag-pickers, and the marginalized people of the suburbs; he dedicated himself to preaching, and to spiritual direction. He promoted the Roman liturgy, and made some effort to enrich the spiritual life of priests through the Eucharist. All his activities sprang from the Eucharist, were motivated by the Eucharist, and aimed to make the Eucharist better known.

In April 1864, the feminine branch was established as a canonical community in Angers under the guidance of Bishop Angebault. Marguerite Guillot, now called Mother Marguerite, was its first superior general. The foundation took place on May 26, 1864.

Fascinated by the Eucharist, Father Eymard affirmed: "*The Holy Eucharist is Jesus, past, present and future*" (PG 356,1). He longed to penetrate its secrets, to open his heart to the rich interior spirit of the Gospel of John which he frequently meditated upon: "Whoever eats my flesh and drinks my blood abides in me and I in him." (Jn. 6:56). The time which he spent in adoration bore fruit in his ministry; he was imbued with new dynamism and strength. His vision of the Eucharist continued to evolve, and especially to become alive in him.

A deeper interior journey led him to a spiritual summit: to the "vow of his personality", the gift of himself (March 21, 1865). Father Eymard let himself be fashioned by the Holy Spirit so that Christ could live in him. (cf. Gal. 2:20), to become Eucharist, " a tasty bread" for the life of his brethren. Everything witnesses to the fact that the Eucharist had become the passion of his life, a passion of love, as he himself said in a sermon:

> *Have a Eucharistic passion. Love like a man who loves someone passionately [...] Whoever sees our Lord in the blessed Sacrament, whoever sees him and is delighted, will turn his mind to our Lord. His thoughts will follow; he will know him, contemplate him; he will see his self-giving love, and, will enter in wonder into the depths of that love. (PR 124,1)*

Father Eymard's final years were marked by illness and every kind of suffering: financial problems, conflicts, misunderstandings, humiliations, loss of the respect of Bishops, the spiritual night. In spite of this, his words remained as ardent as fire and his letters of spiritual direction full of invitations to joy and thanksgiving for God's blessings; he worked tirelessly to the point of exhaustion. The Blessed Sacrament was always dominant in his life: "*The greatest grace of my life has been a keen faith in the Blessed Sacrament*" (Retreat of Saint-Maurice 1868); he saw himself simply as "*God's day-laborer.*"

Peter Julian Eymard died on August 1, 1868, in his native city of La Mure. The Church was on the threshold of Vatican Council I. The epitaph on his tombstone transmits his message to us: "Let us love Jesus, who loves us so in His divine Sacrament."

HAPPY THOSE WHO BELIEVE ...IN THE EUCHARIST

On December 9, 1962 Pope John XXIII proclaimed Peter Julian Eymard a "saint". It was at the end of the first session of Vatican Council II. In his homily on that occasion the pope said: "His characteristic distinction, the guiding thought of all his priestly activities, one may say, was the Eucharist: Eucharistic worship and apostolate."

Peter Julian Eymard was, in his own words, "*always on the way*" as he has been a diocesan priest, a Marist religious, and founder of two religious congregations.

He stressed the importance of baptism, and saw it as the cornerstone of his life and Eucharistic vocation; he was imbued with the Word of God and quoted from it frequently; it was his daily fare.

As he discovered the love of God, it brought about a turning point, an important passage in his life-vision and marked his spirituality; he passed from a spirituality centered on penance and the fear of God to a spirituality centered on God's love.

His eucharistic vocation gradually became clearer, step by step. As Founder of the Congregations of the Religious and of the Servants of the Blessed Sacrament, Father Eymard tried to join together the contemplative and the active life, adoration and apostolate. He saw the Eucharist as the sacrament of the presence of Christ, the mystery of the whole Christ, the summary of his mortal and glorious life, but also as prayer, adoration, sacrifice, communion, Bread of life for individuals and nations, a strength of renewal and transformation for society.

Attentive to the signs of the times and to the situations he met, Father Eymard was able to dialogue with every type of person: workers, youth, aristocrats, the poor, men and women, etc.

He saw the great importance of Eucharistic communion. It was thanks to this communion that he attained the total gift of himself, thus bringing about the words of St. Paul: "It is not I who live, but Christ who lives in me." (Gal 2:20). He came to a deeper union with Christ and to a life completely transformed in love and through love.

Eymard was far from seeing any disparity between celebration, adoration and mission. He recalled that the celebration and contemplation are an integral part of mission and that mission finds its source and its fulfilment in the Eucharist.

He often used the metaphor of hearth and flame and the symbol of the Cenacle. The Cenacle opens up at the breath of Pentecost so that the Church, a Eucharistic community, may bear the Gospel to all peoples. "May your Kingdom come", is the final message which Father Eymard shared with us; he encouraged us to work for a new evangelisation.

These pages are guided by one conviction: though Father Eymard was dependent on the theology of his time, certain intuitions of his anticipated Vatican II, and the insights of the Council enlighten certain values contained in his message.

REFERENCES

Vatican Council II

AA *Apostolicam Acuositatem*, Decree on the lay apostolate, 1965

DV *Dei Verbum* , Dogmatic Constitution on divine Revelation, 1965

LG *Lumen Gentium*, Dogmatic Constitution on the Church, 1964

PrOr *Presbyterium Ordinis*, Decree on Priestly Life and Ministry, 1965

SC *Sacrosanctum Concilium*, Constitution on divine Liturgy, 1963

The Popes

EE John-Paul II, *Ecclesia de Eucharistia*, Encyclical, 2003

SaCa Benedict XVI, *Sacramentum Caritatis*, Apostolic Exhortation, 2007

CCC *Catechism of the Catholic Church*, 1998

Peter Julian Eymard, Complete Works, (French) 2008

CO	Correspondence
CO*	English translation of the Correspondence
NP	Personal Notes
NR	Notes of Personal Retreats
NV	Notes of the "Vade Mecum"
PA	Preaching to religious communities
PC	Preaching to first communicants
PD	Preaching for various groups
PE	Preaching to clergy
PG	Preaching to the Public
PM	Preaching to the Marist Society
PO	Preaching for octaves, novenas, triduums
PP	Public Sermons
PR	Preaching to the Religious of the Blessed Sacrament
PS	Preaching to the Servants of the Blessed Sacrament
PT	Preaching to the Third Order of Mary
RA	Rules for the Aggregation of the Blessed Sacrament
RR	Rules and Constitutions of the Religious of the Blessed Sacrament
RS	Rules and Constitutions of the Servants of the Blessed Sacrament
RT	Rules of the Third Order of Mary

"THE GRATUITOUS AND MERCIFUL GIFT OF HOLY BAPTISM"

"I made my meditation on the gratuitous and all-merciful grace of the Holy Baptism I received. I understood what it is: a new creation in our Lord Jesus Christ, a second life in Jesus Christ, but in Jesus crucified. (Gal 3; 27) [...] I saw the immense graces that made up the dowry of my Baptism:- a child of God, - a member of Jesus Christ, a child of the Church, a brother of the Saints, - a right to the graces and to the glory of Jesus Christ.(Feb. 5, 1865 NR 44, 21)

Peter Julian Eymard was born on February 4, 1811. He was brought to the parish church, and baptised by the pastor, Abbé Joseph Second, on the following day, February 5th.

Whenever he would return to his native town, he never failed to venerate the baptismal font at the parish, just as he also loved to celebrate the anniversary of his baptism and to remind his godmother, his sister Marianne, about the event.

Father Eymard is known as an eminent apostle of the Eucharist and we know how carefully he prepared for his first communion; yet it is surprising to discover that, in his correspondence, he never spoke about the anniversary of his first communion while he would often recall the day of his baptism.

He first began to do this in 1841, two years after his entrance in the society of Marists. At a retreat on February of that year, he noted February 5th to be the feast of St. Agatha and the date of his baptism (cf. NR 15,2). The preceding day, after reciting the *Veni Creator* at the feet of Jesus in the Blessed Sacrament and placing himself under the protection of Mary, he had resolved to make this retreat "*with fervor and fidelity as if it were to be his last.*"

He often wrote letters to his sister Marianne. He expressed his feelings of gratitude as her "godson" for the spiritual support she had given him. He said that he owed his "*vocation to the priesthood*" (CO 17-18*) to her. This underscores the importance and the role of the transmission of the faith in Christian life.

On the anniversary of his baptism, he wrote – "*It is such a beautiful day for me, the most beautiful day of my life.*" (CO 68). This day is also an opportunity to evaluate his life-journey, to remember the positive habits he had acquired especially regarding his religious practices, to pray for his family, his parents, his godfather and godmother. The recollection of his baptism also awakened in him the desire for a life more faithful to God's call, for "*that holiness which is the goal of baptism*" and for "*the love of Jesus Christ in the blessed Sacrament.*" (NR 21).

As Peter Julian Eymard remembered the day of his baptism with a deep sense of gratitude for this "*great grace*" (CO 68-69*), he was also referring, as we have just said, to his vocation to " *the priestly state*".

The passage which has introduced our first day of reflections is taken from a meditation written on February 5th 1865; after recalling the graces which flowed from his baptism, Father Eymard mentioned his three vocations: the vocation to a fervent christian life, to the priestly life and to the religious life, all of which stem from the initial foundation of baptism.

In the same meditation, he quoted St. Francis of Assisi, St. Dominic, St. Ignatius and St. Alphonsus, all founders of religious families. He wrote: "I *received the same graces.*" We can conclude that

Father Eymard also saw his vocation as a founder to be related to his baptismal grace.

In fact, in his second meditation that day, he spoke of the goodness and divine providence of God toward him from the time of his baptism. God had journeyed with him as with St. Paul. Comparing himself to Jacob "always *on the way*", he recalled the different stages of his Eucharistic vocation, which led him to the foundation of the Congregation of the Blessed Sacrament. He spoke of his stay with the Oblates of Mary Immaculate, his Marist experience, and finally of the foundation of the Congregation of the Blessed Sacrament (cf. NR 44,22).

Father Eymard saw baptism as the cornerstone of his whole life and of his vocations. He considered that the spiritual life of every person consists in the development of a new and evangelical life, which is received at the outset by incorporating oneself in the paschal mystery by faith and baptism. Christian maturity consists in an ever-growing participation in the love of Christ for his Father and ours.

In fact, baptism is "the basis of the whole Christian life, the gateway of life in the Spirit" (CCC 1213). Every Christian vocation is rooted in baptism. Baptised persons are "living stones" for the "edification of a spiritual building, for a holy priesthood" (1P: 5). By baptism, they share in the priesthood of Christ, in his prophetic and royal mission.

Father Eymard sought to transmit this conviction to the laity whom he wished to associate to his Congregations' mission. An example of this can be found in a text drawn from the Directory for the Aggregation:

> "*The Christian's grace is foremost a grace of adoption, of divine sonship, a grace of love. It is first of all a grace of feeling which the divine goodness places as a seed in our hearts, and which at baptism shapes the background of the Christian character; this love will then develop with faith, grow with the virtues it inspires and perfects and so become a way of life, a state of love* (RA 18:6)."

The life which is born in us through baptism is a life of love. "*Love is the kingdom of God in the human person*"(RA 18:7). It offers us an entry into the life of the Trinity.

A final passage of Father Eymard's life can be seen as the fulfillment of his baptismal journey.

During the Retreat of Saint-Maurice (April 27 - May 2, 1868), which took place three months before his death, Father Eymard reflected once more on his Eucharistic vocation, on how his life's journey had always been marked by the love of God, and was also marked by a whole series of "*symbolic deaths*"; for example: the separation from the Marist congregation, the problem of the lack of vocations, the departure of his first companion, a "night of the spirit" which lasted at least two years, etc.

At the conclusion of this impressive list, he spoke of the paschal mystery, the power of the Risen Christ, which enlightened Father Eymard's whole existence. From a baptismal point of view, life has the final word; all these "deaths" become passages to Life. Father Eymard proclaims: "*Yet, life follows death; it is the way of the Society and mine*" (NR 45:4).

Baptism is a sharing in the death and resurrection of Jesus Christ. This same mystery is constantly at work in us, our whole life is a passage through death leading towards the resurrection, a new life in Jesus Christ.

TO BE THE WORD OF CHRIST FOR MY BRETHREN AND FOR MY NEIGHBOR

[Our Lord] was the Word of the Father, [cf. Rev. 19:13]. He repeated this divine word with respect, it was divine, holy. He repeated the divine word with love, for it was a grace [...] The word of Jesus Christ is spirit and life [Jn.6:63] it is all-powerful. If My words abide in you, ask whatever you will and it shall be done for you [Jn.15:7]. He spoke and it came to be [Ps 33:9]. The words of Jesus Christ were the rays of this sun of truth. I am the light of the world [Jn.8:12]. They were light in the midst of darkness [...] That is what I must be for my brethren and for my neighbor, the word of Christ [cf. Col.3:16]. (NR 44,63).

Today the word of God holds a very important place in the life of our Christian communities and of every disciple of Jesus Christ. In October 2008, the Church convoked a synod on the theme: "The Word of God in the life and mission of the Church." In fact, the Church is founded on the Word of God, is born from it and lives by it.

In Father Eymard's time, the Word of God was not given much importance, especially in the Catholic Church, whilst we can affirm that Father Eymard's life was regularly nurtured with the Word of God. He systematically quoted the Scriptures in his writings, in his notes, in his preaching. He was quite versed in the Word of God. He can be seen as a mystic nourished by the Word of God.

On March 2, 1861, at the time of his annual retreat, he wrote: "*Let us thank our Lord Jesus Christ for all the graces which he has showered upon us to this very day, and in particular for having received his divine word"(PR 12,1).* And again: "*the word of God is a grace, and one of the greatest graces"(PG 17:3).*

Father Eymard was always careful to listen to God [speaking] in his Word. This attentiveness to God, speaking through the Scriptures, was already evident from the outset of his priestly ministry. He noted: "*A priest who lets a day go by without reading the Scriptures has lost his day" (NR 9,7).*

As a young parochial vicar, he set up a reading

plan for the Sacred Scriptures which he followed using the Vulgate: every book of the Bible would be read from beginning to end, the Old and New Testaments read simultaneously, three chapters from the Old and one from the New. A notebook was kept alongside this reading to jot down whatever difficulties would be encountered, with solutions to be sought at a later time (cf. NV 3,33).

A word of advice from that period seems very interesting. Father Eymard wrote: *All of Scripture must be read in the same spirit in which it was dictated"(NV 3,34).* This exhortation resembles a text from the Constitution on Revelation from Vatican II: "The Sacred Scriptures must be read and interpreted in the same Spirit which inspired them."*(DV 12).*

After his entrance with the Marists, when Father Eymard carried the Blessed Sacrament during the procession of Corpus Christi on May 25, 1845, he asked the Lord to give him the spirit of the letters of St. Paul, *"that great lover of Jesus Christ,"* and he promised to read at least two chapters a day.

The Word of God also held a place of pride in the advice he would give to his directees. He invited them to read Sacred Scriptures "*a little more often*" (cf. CO 1323), and come to love them; in fact, " *this reading helps the soul aspire towards God, feeds it, keeps it delightfully occupied"* (CO 1859-1860*).

The Word of God truly nourished Father Eymard's spiritual journey. The text which we are proposing for this second day is from a meditation of February 24, 1865, and took place in a specific context.

Father Eymard was in Rome to handle the important question of purchasing the building considered to be the place of the cenacle of Jerusalem. He had come to ask permission to establish a community of the Congregation at the very place where, according to tradition, the Eucharist had been instituted.

As the matter was continually postponed, Father Eymard used the time at his disposal for a personal spiritual retreat and decided to withdraw to the Redemptorist Fathers, near St. Mary Major, where he would stay sixty-five days.

A text from the liturgy of the day, January 25th, the feast of the conversion of St. Paul, served to open his retreat. The Word of God of that day became his point of entry: "*What must I do, Lord?*" (Act. 22,11). He set about listening to the Holy Spirit speaking in his life.

We can see a double movement, a sort of "to and fro." Sometimes Father Eymard would use a text from Scripture as his starting point of meditation and sometimes the Word of God would confirm his own intuitions. At other times, he brought several texts together for a single theme. He was nourished by the Word which he quoted from memory. The texts most often used were: the Psalms, Isaiah, the Gospels, especially St. John and St. Paul.

Aside from St. Paul, other archetypes enlightened his path: Abraham leaving his country and ready to sacrifice his son Isaac; Jacob always on the way; the Servant of God; the family of Nazareth; Mary in the Incarnation and St. Joseph, father, guide and protector; the 144,000 who follow the Lamb to Mount Sion.

The Word of God is Jesus-Christ, he himself is the Word, the Word of the Father (cf. Rev.19:13). He transmitted this divine and holy Word with love; this word is a grace, it is "spirit and life"(cf. Jn. 6:63), it sanctifies the world, recreates it, sets it ablaze like a fire burning in one's heart (cf. Lk. 24:32). It is a light and this word shall one day finally judge the world (cf. NR 44,63).

One witness affirmed that Father Eymard's respect for the Sacred Scriptures was outstanding: "He always carried the Gospel of John on himself". Father Eymard did not feel that it was enough to listen to God and his Word, but thanks to the action of the Holy Spirit, he understood that he should let this word dwell in him until he would become transformed by it and himself become a word of Christ for others:

That is what I must be for my brethren and for my neighbor, the word of Christ [cf. Col 3:16]. That is what the apostles were.. You yourselves will not be the speakers, the spirit of your Father will speak in you [Mt.10:20] (NR 44,63).

Today the method of "lectio divina" has become a common practice once again. One step of this method is called "contemplation, or pondering". Though Father Eymard did not know this method, yet in a meditation to the Servants of the Blessed Sacrament he invited them "to ponder" upon [Scripture].

"We must always ponder [...] Notice what Our Lord said at the Last Supper: If you abide in me, and my words abide in you, if you ponder them, digest them, all that you wish shall be done [cf.Jn.15,7]. What! Yes, look at the Virgin Mary: And Mary kept all these things in her heart [cf. Lc2:19,51]. That is, [see]his actions and his words and meditate upon them, contemplate them, delight in them in one's heart, whatever you wish, for the word of God is life-giving, and we must take hold of it (PS 641,8).

THE LOVE OF GOD AND THE WINGS OF THE ROYAL EAGLE

"Imagine perfection as a high mountain and the Christian being told: "You must climb to [the summit of] the mountain of God." There are difficulties and sacrifices along the way, as he climbs, he slips and falls; there are so many difficulties on the way to perfection! Another person [...] takes wings and flies. The first one walks, exercising virtues, working out perfection to the smallest detail. This is long, very long, he does not make much progress, he will only reach perfection at the end of his life. The other is St. John, the beloved disciple, he flies like an eagle [cf. Rv. 4:7) with the wings of love. He reaches the summit of the mountain to contemplate our Lord Jesus Christ, his beauty, his goodness, his graciousness. He speaks with him and sees what he has done for the love of mankind. He wants to know him, to serve and love him. He begins by looking at him, and then he loves him and offers himself to him. (PS 321).

Father Eymard's youth was marked by a spirituality of penance and reparation. The current of Jansenistic thought which was still prevalent in that region had impressed him with the image of a punishing God and with a feeling of human unworthiness.

It was in that spirit that the child Peter Julian would often go barefoot even on the snow to visit the Calvary at the edge of town to prepare himself for his first communion. One experience, however, would profoundly mark the life of Father Eymard, and bring about a radical change in his spiritual journey: the liberating discovery of the love of God.

Father Eymard's first assignment was as a vicar at Chatte (1834-1837). He would accompany his pastor to St. Romans when the latter visited the neighboring pastor. Father Eymard would leave the two to their conversation and walk to the promontory in the village cemetery to pray and meditate in solitude.

This place was known as the "Rock of St. Romans." Its chapel, the beauty of nature, the silence and peace of the valleys and hills, the place itself hold the secret which brought Father Eymard to a deeper knowledge of the love of God. When he told Mme Jordan (a woman whose summer home was in the region) about his experience there, "*at the setting of a beautiful day*", he highlighted the goodness and personal love of God primarily shown through nature:

> *The soul loves hills and mountains. It feels like it is touching Heaven from there, and closer to God. You are fortunate to see those beautiful peaceful mountains. The soul rises higher because of them. You are happy in the countryside alone with God, with the purity of nature and the beauty of divine Providence. (CO 845- 846*)*

Nature is a book which is "*excellent and ever new,*" which we must read continually; a book of love which God has written on every plant, on every grain of sand, and within yourself. Father Eymard calls us *to honor this beautiful book and to add a few pages of gratitude and love*". We can interpret our life experience in the light of this book of love and come to a deeper and more intimate knowledge of God. (cf. CO 971 – 972*).

With the passage of time, the meaning of his experience at Saint -Romans took on a greater depth and the rock became his "*mystical rock*", which brought him closer to God, even to "*delight in God*" and to " *lose oneself a little in the harmony of his heart*". (CO 1380-1379*).

Prayer is changed into contemplation where the

soul nourishes itself on God, on his personal love and tenderness. Astonished, in awe of this love, the soul wonders what it can do for God to correspond to such great love.

Every aspect of life becomes a locus which reveals the love of God:

> *The secret of this simple view is to see things at first glance under the aspect of God's goodness for us, the reason for this grace, what it cost our Lord, its reality and permanence for us. When the soul has the joy of finding this good side, prayer becomes more like a delightful contemplation, where the hour passes quickly. Oh! dear daughter, how often do I wish and desire that you may taste God in this way! It lasts a long time; that is my rock of St. Romans! (CO 2011)*

The metaphor of the mountain, which described the experience of Saint-Romans is found again during the Great Retreat of Rome (1865); Father Eymard had reached the *"mountain of love!"* where he could contemplate " *the God of Love*".

God loves us with an eternal love, a Father's love, a tender love; he loves us *personally with a great benevolent love, an infinite love*". (CO 1538-1535*). The Incarnation of Jesus Christ is the most evident proof of it. God " *became man like us to become our brother in the flesh [...] and he became poor, the poorest* *of the poor, in order to embrace us all as his brethren".*

God loves us and gives us all that he is and all that he has. *The Father has given his Son, the Son has given his very self. The Holy Spirit has become our regular sanctifier."*

God loves us and this love finds it summit in the Eucharist.

> *Our Lord loves us so much that he cannot separate himself from us, not even in his state of glory. … Oh! if only we truly understood the love of God! The love of Jesus in his birth, his suffering, his sacrament! It would be enough to die of gratitude or contrition. (NR 44, 102).*

Love is not an isolated act of virtue, love "*is a life*", says Father Eymard, just as it was the human and divine life of Jesus Christ (cf. NR 44, 129). Jesus Christ, the Word made flesh is love made tangible, incarnate. All that he said was spoken through love, all that he did was the fruit of love. And after having shown love to his disciples, he gave them love: the Eucharist (cf. PS 321).

The experience of Saint-Romans allowed Father Eymard to undertake a journey which led him to a concept of religion inspired by love. This became his own path. "*Love! That is my law, my path, my virtue, my strength, my joy, my happiness, my life, my death, my heaven! Amen!*" (NR 44,111).

This experience was transmitted to his institutes. He proposed the primacy of love as the "*characteristic and distinctive way*" for his men and women religious. The article [in the Rule] explaining the spirit of his congregations is the same for both the masculine and feminine congregations:

The law and spirit of divine love will be the inspiration and the supreme law of their lives and the bond of union among them as among the members of the same body, so that vivified by this love, having only one heart to serve him, they may consecrate themselves entirely to the greater glory of our Lord Jesus in his Sacrament. (RR 78,1 and RS 14, 1)

Father Eymard proposed the way of " royal love" as the shortest and most noble way for the laity as well. This way gives the "wings of the royal eagle" to all, in order to soar to God himself (RA 16,2), 18,2). *Oh! Blessed is the soul who walks Jesus' way of perfection by the way of royal love. She runs, she flies, with the strength of a royal eagle. (PD 22)*

"A LIVELY FAITH" IN THE EUCHARIST

"Let the Holy Eucharist be your starting point; just as the rays all emanate from the sun, in the same way, this hearth of all light will be your point of departure. The holy Eucharist is Jesus past, present and future. It was the loving purpose of his mortal life. All the mysteries are glorified therein, all his virtues admirably continued; it is the sovereign mystery of faith where all truths converge like rivers into the ocean which feeds them. When we have said Eucharist, we have said everything! It is Jesus in his sacramental state! But, in order that the Eucharist may radiate everywhere, it must be our life's inspiration, the royal science of our mind, our heart's sovereign love; then it will become our life's noble passion. Our life is fully defined by our dominant passion." (PG 356,1).

Toward the end of his life, Father Eymard wrote: "*we have known the love of God for us, and we have believed in it* [...] *Happy those who believe in love, who believe in the Eucharist.*" (PO 37,1). This affirmation followed by just a few days these other words written in his retreat notes: *The greatest grace of my life was a lively faith in the blessed Sacrament, even from my youth." (NR 45,3).*

This kind of faith in the real presence of Christ in the Eucharist was a constant factor in Father Eymard's life. As a child, he often visited the Blessed Sacrament, like a friend often visits a friend (cf. NR 3,6). On the day of his first communion he promised to become a priest. He had to take it one step at a time before the Eucharist would definitively become his center of life and action.

Father Eymard spoke of the Eucharist as the greatest grace of his life. The word "grace" was also used to indicate other moments in his life. He spoke for example, of a grace of vocation, a grace of self-giving, of union, of happiness (cf. NR 45,3).

We must not understand this word "grace" to mean a miracle, a vision or something extraordinary, but rather a strong interior movement, an attraction which moved his spirit, which developed and matured within him, which had originated in the spiritual encounters and experiences which marked his journey.

On November 1844, Father Colin, the founder of the Marist Fathers, called him to Lyons to work at his side. This period turned out to be a rich and fruitful time for his apostolic ministry and his spiritual progress, because it brought him to live in the midst of economic, industrial, cultural and religious revolution.

In Lyons, he formed friendships with the Cure d'Ars and Pauline Jaricot, Marguerite Guillot and the members of the Third Order of Mary, Camille Rambaud who had begun a project for the education of poor children, and Father Chevrier; the philosopher M. Blanc de Saint Bonnet and the "*mystical school of Lyons*", composed of young inquirers (artists and writers), seeking inspiration from the gospel of St. John. He was in contact with the founders of institutes such as Marcellin Champagnat, the founder of the Marist Brothers, Brother Gabriel Tabourin, founder of the Brothers of the Holy Family of Belley, and Theodelinde Dubouché, foundress of Adoration Réparatrice. His assignment to prepare the departure of missionaries for Oceania instilled him with their missionary spirit, including a desire for martyrdom. He read the letters of Marie-Eustelle Harpain (1814-1842), a young mystic, " *a saintly lover of the divine Eucharist*"(CO 1163-1164*).

Other events were decisive in giving direction to Father Eymard's spiritual life:

On May 25, 1845 his attraction was confirmed at the church of Saint-Paul in Lyons: to preach Jesus-Christ and Jesus Christ Eucharistic. He chose St. Paul, this great lover of Jesus Christ, as his patron and from that time onward, longed to bring the faithful to Christ's Eucharistic presence through his ministry.

On January 21, 1851, while praying at Notre Dame de Fourvière, he was deeply concerned by the spiritual neglect of the laity and priests and their lack of devotion toward this holy Sacrament. A very strong thought emerged: a conviction of his vocation to make the Eucharist known, the mystery of love, to regenerate the Catholic world especially by means of adoration, and to create a group of men in order to do so. He wrote:

> *"I have often reflected upon the remedies for the universal indifference which is talking hold of so many Catholics in a frightening manner, and I find only one: the Eucharist" (CO 286).*

During the month of September 1851, Father Eymard left Lyons bringing this call with him in his heart. It would be at La Seyne-sur-Mer on April 18, 1853, when another stronger call indicated the meaning of his vocation: to devote himself to the service of the Blessed Sacrament, to find means to support and form the great Work of perpetual Adoration, to establish the religious order of the Blessed Sacrament (cf. CO 412- 415*).

There was a military port at Toulon near to La Seyne. Captain Raymond de Cuers, who would be Father Eymard's first companion in the Congregation of the Blessed Sacrament was stationed there and had already gathered together a group of young men in view of founding a new Order dedicated to perpetual Adoration.

Father Eymard, heedful of the social problems of his times, felt that the Church of his times was not responding sufficiently to the spiritual needs of the faithful. This led him to question and wonder:

> *"Now we must quickly get to work, to save souls through the divine Eucharist, to awaken France and Europe numbed in dormant apathy because they don't know the gift of God, Jesus the Eucharistic Emmanuel. (CO 325)*

Father Eymard was the first to dedicate himself to it and wanted to engage others to work with him. He wanted to reveal the Eucharist to those who did not know about it, help them to find a radiant center for their lives: the Eucharist. The presence of the risen Christ in the Eucharist, is an active presence, it can rekindle love and be the source of an authentic Christian life.

At the end of a difficult discernment, he asked Father Favre, the superior general of the Marists, to free him from his vows so that he could dedicate himself to the work to which he felt called: to found a congregation of men vowed to the Eucharist. On April 30, 1856, he went to Paris to submit his project to the Archbishop, Mgr. Sibour. This latter was diffident toward a work that he judged to be purely contemplative but he agreed with it on May 13, 1856 because of the commitment to prepare adults for first communion. And so, the Congregation of the Blessed Sacrament was founded.

It was clear to Father Eymard from the beginning that his congregation would unite the active to the contemplative life, and that the Eucharistic life is a life committed to the salvation of mankind. The Eucharist and society cannot be two separate realities.

> *We have only one thought, one goal, one center: The Eucharist! How happy if we could become special men, and bring back the selfish and indifferent men of our poor society to faith and love toward the Eucharist. (CO 609- 611*).*

"THE HEARTH HAS A FLAME"

I have come [to cast] fire [on earth] [Lk 12:49]. What is this fire that Jesus Christ brings from heaven to earth? That he desires so ardently to enkindle everywhere? This heavenly, mysterious fire is divine love – for God is love, and whoever abides in love abides in God and God in him [cf. 1Jn. 4:12–13]. But where does this divine fire reside? Where is its home? Saint John Chrysostom replies: the source of love is the Eucharist […]That is where the love of Jesus Christ stirs us, penetrates us, sets us on fire […] Come to this perpetual fire which Jesus Christ has enkindled on the altar, come to warm your lethargic faith, revive your devotion, rekindle your love which may have cooled, and you will personally experience the substance and power of this fire, the love of Jesus Christ in the blessed Sacrament (PG 283,1).

At the time of the canonization of Father Eymard (December 1962), the Bishop of Grenoble, Bishop Fougerat, declared that the originality of his message consisted in his wanting at any price, to unite the Eucharist of contemplative- adorers and the Eucharist of apostle-missionaries. He called Father Eymard the "man of wholeness."

In fact, on the day following the foundation of the Congregation of the Blessed Sacrament, he affirmed that he wanted *"to embrace the Eucharistic in its every aspect"* (CO 553-557*) "*We take the whole Eucharist*" (CO 690-693*).

Father Eymard saw the Eucharist as the sacrament *par excellence* of God's love, the supreme act of love of Jesus Christ for humanity, a love which combines all loves, the gift crowning all gifts, the grace of graces.

He was convinced of the centrality, strength and dynamism of this mystery. "*A purely contemplative life cannot be fully Eucharistic: the hearth has a flame.*" (CO 1030 -1032*). This passionate love of Jesus Christ must be welcomed and shared. The Eucharist "*shows us the love of Jesus Christ for mankind and inspires us with a great love for Jesus Christ*"(PG 144,1).

The metaphor of fire, of the hearth and flame, expresses his Eucharistic passion very well. The inspiration for this metaphor came from the Gospel (Lk. 12:49): "I have come to light a fire upon the earth, how I wish the blaze was ignited!" and by St. John Chrysostom ("The Eucharist is an ember which sets us on fire.").

As the fire has a flame, so love for God is completed with love for one's neighbor. First of all this fire must fill and burn in all hearts. That is why the religious are to begin with ardent prayer at the feet of the God of love and once enkindled go to spread his glory and extend his reign [to others]. Father Eymard spoke of courageous men: "*firebrands of the Eucharistic fire*". (cf. PR 149,11)

This image implies a living dynamism, which encompasses all of life. Father Eymard proposed a spirituality nurtured on the celebration and contemplation of the Eucharist and dedicated to the service of the Gospel, particularly in favor of the most disadvantaged.

The fruitful tension between these two poles is without any division, as hearth and flame cannot be separated. He noted in his Great Retreat of Rome, "*An adorer who is also an apostle should always adore and preach Jesus Hostia*" (NR 44,136).

The inspiration is clear: For Father Eymard, everything flows from the Eucharist and returns to it. The Eucharist, he affirmed, "*is our center of life, our strength in action and apostolate*" (PR 107,3). He did not give any details concerning the apostolate. He spoke of works, writings and preachings: to adore, to love and serve Jesus Christ in the divine Eucharist; to make it known to those who do not yet know him and to reveal it more extensively to those who already know him, by means of catechesis, retreats and gatherings. He spoke of fighting by the fire of the Eucharist the indifference which reigns in the world, to show the love of Jesus Christ in order to awaken faith and love. In a word, "*whatever can procure the glory of the God of the Eucharist*" (PR 149,11).

If we consider Father Eymard's constant activity and all that he accomplished, the multiple initiatives which he set in place given his fragile health, to embody his charism, his Eucharistic grace, we can grasp the passion which animated him and which should stimulate our own creativity for the Eucharistic mission.

Father Eymard perceived that the Eucharist constitutes a power of renewal for the Church and society. He invites us to share in his own passion for the Eucharist.

Until we have a passionate love for the Eucharist, we will not have done anything for God. [...] Have a Eucharistic passion, love like someone who loves another passionately (PR 24,1).

He continually deepened his faith and understanding of the Eucharistic mystery. He meditated on the Scriptures, particularly the gospel of St. John. He was an avid reader (the Church Fathers, theologians, spiritual authors and the decrees of the Council of Trent on the Eucharist). He spent hours in prayer and in contemplation of Christ in the Eucharist. For Father Eymard, the Eucharist was the sacrament of Christ's presence, the mystery of the whole Christ, the summary of his mortal and glorious life. " *The holy Eucharist is Jesus past, present and future*" (PG 356,1). It contains the whole spiritual treasure of the Church. Vatican II would say," Christ himself, our Passover, the living bread"(PrOr 5).

A text summarizes well his vision of the Eucharistic mystery:

"Since among all pious works, the holy Sacrifice of the Mass and communion to the Body of our Lord Jesus Christ constitute without any doubt the purpose and vitality of the whole of religion, let each one worthily cultivate and develop their devotion toward this mystery so divine, let them direct their virtue and love [to it] like means toward its goal" (RR 74t,6).

We don't know whether this text is from Father Eymard himself or whether he copied it from some other author. What is sure, is that he adopted this vision as his own. He seemed convinced that the sacrifice of the Mass and sacramental communion continue to be the vital source and the summit of the entire religion. The Mass is:

> "...*the Eucharistic wonder which summarizes all the others, and which, by itself alone equals all the love, sacrifices, and glory which our Savior offered to his Father during his mortal life PG 244,4).*

If the whole Christian life is to bear fruit, it must begin from Jesus Christ and return to him, be nourished and centered on the Eucharist (cf. PG 241,5).

This centrality of the Eucharistic celebration foretold, a century beforehand, the teaching of Vatican II. (cf. SC 10).

As he drew near to the end of his life, he wrote the following : " *Grace of the apostolate: faith in Jesus. Jesus is there, so then, [all] to him, through Him, in Him.*" (NR 45). This phrase brings to mind the doxology of the Eucharistic prayer. Father Eymard understood that the presence of Christ in the Eucharist is at the source of endless dynamism and mission.

"TO MAKE ADORATION THE CENTER OF MY LIFE"

To adore Jesus Christ in the blessed Sacrament is to know him, like Saint Thomas, as our Lord and God [cf.Jn20:28], to bow at his feet like the man born blind, worshiping his visible body with the public confession of his hidden divinity [cf. Jn9:30-33]. [...] to adore Jesus Christ in the blessed Sacrament is to adore his greatness, the tenderness of his love for humanity, which was preparing, instituting and perpetuating the holy Eucharist, to be the perpetual victim of salvation, the heavenly bread, and the consolation of our earthly pilgrimage. Finally, to adore Jesus Christ in his sacrament is to make the holy Eucharist the purpose of our life, the goal of our devotion, the purpose of our virtues, the loving object of all our sacrifices. (RA 23,7)

Aware of the pastoral challenges of his time, particularly of its unbelief, rationalism and materialism, Father Eymard wanted to bring the faithful back to the person of Jesus, the source of life, to let them encounter his love (*"They no longer know him as their neighbor, friend and God" PG 241,4)* in the mystery of the Eucharist by means of adoration.

He lived the Eucharist fully; his life of adoration fed his apostolic ministry and this nurtured his life of adoration. During his final retreat (1868) he wrote in his notes:

> *To make of adoration the pivot of my life, to prepare my adorations as one prepares a meal, an important address. The soul of my adorations: the gift of self" (NR 45, 16).*

Eucharistic adoration was also proposed as the *pivot* of the congregations he founded. It was to be their characteristic form of prayer, their mission and their *grace*. This practice, in the context of solemn exposition of the blessed Sacrament was to be a proclamation of faith by the men and women religious, and a witness to their devotion and love for Christ present in the Sacrament of the altar.

Father Eymard wanted adoration to be experienced according to the spirit of the Church; in fact, the adorer prays as a delegate of the Church.

He did not leave this to chance, but provided it with a structure, rules and guidelines, in order that adoration be well prepared as we would prepare a meal or a discourse.

He proposed a simple and practical method to strengthen and nurture the prayer of adoration for both religious and laity: adoration according to the four ends of sacrifice (that is, the spirit of the Church in the celebration of the Mass). During an hour, one should consecrate a quarter hour to adoration, a quarter hour to giving thanks, a quarter hour to ask forgiveness, and finally a quarter hour to intercede for the Church and the world. (cf. RR 78,4)

This method connects adoration to the Eucharistic celebration, for it introduces one into the movement of the celebration itself and into the attitudes of Christ instituting the Eucharist.

The documents of the magisterium of the Church recall the importance of this relationship between celebration and adoration: the instruction *Eucharisticum Mysterium* (May 25, 1967), the Ritual for the Eucharist outside of Mass (June 21, 1973) and recently Pope John Paul II's encyclical *Ecclesia de Eucharistia*, and Pope Benedict XVI on the occasion of the Synod on the Eucharist.

According to the proposed method, Eucharistic

adoration makes it possible to enter into the manifold riches of the Eucharistic mystery. Father Eymard said:

> *Do enter into these attitudes: to adore, that is your purpose, adoration, reparation, thanksgiving, prayer; do not stop solely at one of the ends of the sacrifice, but take the four, the whole Eucharist. You have the blessed Sacrament in its entirety in you. (PS 236,8).*

Adoration facilitates a loving knowledge of Jesus Christ (not just something theological or intellectual) who said: "Whoever loves me will be loved by my Father, I will also love him and will manifest myself to him" (Jn. 14:21) This manifestation, according to Father Eymard, takes place through adoration, since the Eucharist is our Lord himself, where we find the breadth, the depth, the length, the height of his love (cf. Eph. 3: 18-19).

In a statement written in 1867, Father Eymard accentuated the importance of the body at prayer, of the human person as a whole and of interior silence; he called for an act of faith to "*open the senses, the heart and the mind to Eucharistic devotion*". Prayer is not [to be] an individual prayer, but done in union with the prayer of Christ and the prayer of the Church; it opens herself to the world (cf. PO 35).

The method proposed is not limited to the time of the celebration, but following the liturgical calendar, it also integrates all the mysteries of the life of Jesus-Christ, the feasts of the Virgin Mary and the saints.

Father Eymard suggests figures from the gospel as examples of prayer and adoration: the kings as being the first adorers; the Samaritan woman who learned how to adore "in spirit and in truth", the man born blind and his journey of faith; Mary of Bethany and her gesture of humility, daring and love; Mary Magdalene and her loving search; and finally, Thomas in his act of total faith " My Lord and My God". Adoration is thus nurtured by the Word of God.

However, the best way to adore the Lord is the one which the Holy Spirit inspires and favors in a humble and simple heart (RR 78,4).

Father Eymard was aware that methods and rules are not sufficient and that the Holy Spirit alone can provide the grace and joy of prayer. It is the Holy Spirit who teaches us to pray, who inspires our prayer and guides it. Each person must therefore pray in union with the Holy Spirit, allow the Spirit to pray in him and through him. Adoration thus acquires a Trinitarian dimension.

"The soul of my adorations: the gift of myself."

Adoration, for Father Eymard, was not just a devotion, an act of worship, but a state of life. The adorer`s whole being, his whole life, must become adoration.

The purpose of adoration is union with Christ, so as to belong to Him, (cf. Rm. 8:9) abide in him (cf. Jn. 6:56) and live for him, to have his spirit and so bring about his reign in the world. "*Everyone who desires to live by Jesus–Christ is necessarily meditative, contemplative, adoring"(PR 8:3).* Jesus Christ forms the adorer, conforming him to himself through the Holy Spirit. "*To become gentle, I will keep my eyes fixed on the Eucharist"*(NR 44, 101), writes Father Eymard.

Therefore, he was teaching us that adoration is connected to the Eucharistic celebration and the liturgical year, nurtured on the Word of God, united to the Holy Spirit and the Church, to lead the world to Christ. He was inviting us to enter into a dynamic movement to make our love mature, thanks to the Eucharist.

> *"Love[...] continues to grow into the mysteries of his grace and love, and when it thinks that it has grasped Jesus fully, it discovers new splendors – "from glory to glory"--[cf. 2Co. 3:18], - and so it is always satisfied and yet always hungry – a representation of heaven, or of a depthless and boundless ocean," (PG 281).*

THE EUCHARIST, "BREAD FOR THE WEAK AND FOR THE STRONG"

"Continue to go to communion because you are weak, and then because we must live in our Lord and receive him in order to do so, because our kind Savior has said: 'Whoever eats me will live for me [Jn. 6:57] the one who eats my flesh and drinks my blood abides in me and I in him.' [Jn. 6:56]. It is better to go to Holy Communion with your weaknesses than to distance yourself from it through fear or humility. Love expresses itself more through surrender than through respect, more through trust than through fear. Receive communion with the desire to love him ever more; that is the best disposition. (CO 240 -243).*

Father Eymard was strongly convinced of the need for sacramental communion in the Christian life. This idea became persistent from the start of the foundation of his congregations and it intensified even further during his final years. He said: *The Eucharist was established in the form of food. The soul must first nourish itself upon it."(PP 67,3).* He said this on July 16th 1868, on the eve of his departure for La Mure, where he was to die on August 1st.

Father Eymard invited people to adore the Lord, but even more, to frequent and even daily communion. His thinking on this point was truly innovative given the era in which he was living, it was based on the Church's Tradition. He wrote:

> *During the first centuries attendance at the holy sacrifice and the reception of communion were seen as two inseparable actions and the pastors of the Church always highly advised to unite them (PG 251,5).*

In the face of objections of those who fear abuses, or of those who think that Communion was a reward for virtue, or of those who deprived themselves of it through humility, Father Eymard reacted firmly and decisively; he spoke of false humility, of an insult to Jesus-Christ who is inviting us to come to his love and who is waiting for us. To those who sought his advice, he wrote:

> *Begin with this principle: the poorer I am, the more I need God (CO 2039 –2042*). Never give up the*

> *daily Communion; that would be like giving up your place at the family feast of God's children. In this matter, we shouldn't consider our unworthiness, nor our dryness, but rather our weakness, the loving invitation of our good Master and the company of our good Mother. (CO 2172).*

The Eucharist is primarily the bread of life, as Jesus tells us in the gospel of St. John. (Jn. 6). It is food, nourishment and strength, the *"traveller's daily bread"* (cf. 1Kings 19:8 and Lk. 11:3), the bread of understanding, the bread of the heart and of love (cf. PP 21,1 and 26, 1).

> *"Jesus has made the Eucharist to be bread for both the weak and the strong, a remedy against sin, a powerful weapon against the devil, the on-going marvel of his resurrection and his life in his infirm and suffering members. Come then toward the Holy Eucharist [...] There, at his feet, you will find grace, strength for good, light and love. [...] Throw all your weaknesses into this divine fire, like a straw being cast into the fire. Plunge your soiled baptismal robe in the pure and true blood of the Lamb of God, and it will emerge white and pure. (PD 19, 23)."*

The Eucharist cannot be dissociated from our baptismal life; if baptism is the starting point of the Christian life, then it follows that we should be nourished, therefore we must receive communion.

Nowadays we say that the Eucharist completes the Christian initiation, it is the center and the end of the sacramental life. (cf. SaCa 1).

According to Father Eymard, communion is necessary for the development of our faith, in order to grow in Christ. Without the Eucharist, Christians cannot be strong or well-formed, "*Our whole formation must be done by Jesus Christ lest it be incomplete.*" (PO 37,4).

The disciples of Emmaus recognized Jesus at the breaking of the bread (cf. Lk. 24:13-35). They needed the Eucharist to penetrate deeply the mystery of Christ. Eucharistic Communion introduces the faithful into a knowledge of the one Lord, which allows him, in some way, to take hold of God in his mystery of infinite love and live by it. This interior knowledge is an irreplaceable Eucharistic grace. At Communion, Jesus comes to reveal himself.

> *"The soul who receives Communion, who had some preliminary idea of Our Lord, sees him, recognizes him at the holy table. We can know Our Lord only through his very self." (PO 37,5).*

At the breaking of bread, the burning heart is enlightened on his situation, it is the law of love which Jesus has placed in our hearts at Communion (cf. Jr. 31:33 and 2 Cor. 3:3). Thanks to the Eucharist we can face the sacrifices of the Christian life, it has [even] sustained martyrs. (cf. PS17:1). It becomes like wings to [to help us]fly, it gives strength, warmth, enthusiasm and generosity:

> *Charity also needs the Eucharist in order to spend itself for one's neighbor. Yes, we need the Eucharist to love our neighbor as Jesus Christ loves us, unto the gift of self, to devote oneself, unto sacrifice, unto death. Thus, we are giving only what Jesus Christ himself has given to us each day. (RA 26,5).*

The Eucharist is Jesus who communicates the very life of God to us:

> *Let him kiss me with the kiss of his mouth [Ct. 1:1]. An early Father of the Church called the Eucharist the gift of a kiss. It is by the Eucharistic kiss that Jesus lets his soul, his spirit, his life and his whole heart flow into us. (NP 60,3).*

Thanks to communion, we are transformed into Jesus who takes flesh, is born, develops and perfects himself in us. In fact he has said: "Whoever eats me will live by me." (Jn. 6:57), and again:"Whoever eats my body and drinks my blood abides in me and I in him" (Jn. 6:56). To the young workers who had just received their first communion, Father Eymard said; "*This morning, you have received communion, that is, Jesus Christ has changed you into himself. You are now one with his body, his blood, his soul, his divinity*". (PC 19,3).

The body of the communicant becomes the place where Christ is present and active; the new life of conformity to Christ by baptism is energized, to the point that we can speak of an on-going incarnation.

> "*That is the wonder of the Eucharist, the marvel of the on-going incarnation in the human person [...] by holy communion the life of the communicant is sacramentally united to that of Jesus Christ and takes on its merit and virtue and comes to such a transformation into Jesus Christ, that it can truly be said as the apostle did: I live [Gal. 2:20]. Communion is therefore the life of Jesus Christ in us (PG 310,1).*"

The Eucharist brings us a great treasure. It is a feast, it is joy of the spirit, peace and happiness; it is the true manna of the desert, a divine food which is as delightful as it is strengthening. It is the body of the Risen Christ which provokes an "*explosion of light and fire in well-disposed hearts*" (PG 242,2). The words of the psalm take on new meaning: "Taste and see: the Lord is good" Ps. 33,9). Finally, the Eucharist heals us, it rehabilitates fallen man; in a word, it divinises us.

THE TOTAL GIFT OF SELF

"It is as if the Savior said:[...] so, by communion, you will live for me, for I shall be living in you. I will fill your soul with my desires and my life which will consume and destroy whatever is proper to you. So much shall it be I who lives and desires everything in you, instead of you. And so, you will be entirely clothed with me. You will be the body of my heart; your heart, the receptacle, the movement of my heart. I will be the person of your personality, and your personality will be the life of mine in you. "It is no longer I who lives, but it is Christ who lives in me." [Gal 2:20] (NR 44,119)."

His " lively faith" toward the Eucharist drew Father Eymard into the movement which led Christ to give his life for the salvation of the world. He never stopped meditating and preaching about this tremendous love which touched him personally:

"He has loved me, he has given himself over for me, love creates identity of life." (NR 44,100) and "love consists in an exchange"(NR 44, 120). This love demands to give all like Christ, who gave himself to us completely, who loved us to the end.

The Holy Spirit led Father Eymard to a final stage, one that was more interior than exterior: the vow of his personality, the total gift of himself.

At the end of a first retreat in Rome, Father Eymard had written: *"I have finally understood that God would rather have an act of my heart, the gift of my person, than any exterior action; that an interior act is more glorious and pleasing to him than all the apostolate in the world." (NR 42,9),* It was Pentecost Sunday May 24, 1863.

Two years later, (1865), in Rome once again, on the occasion of another retreat, the same intuition emerged:

> *"Our Lord showed me that he prefers the gift of my heart to any exterior gifts that I could give him, even if I could give him the hearts of everyone, without giving him my own." (NR 44,29).*

As we already said on the second day, Father Eymard was in Rome for a project which was dear to his heart: to found a community of the Congregation in Jerusalem, if possible in the Cenacle itself, the place where Jesus instituted the Eucharist. As the question was dragging on, he used the time at his disposal for a spiritual retreat.

This retreat can almost be read as an on-going dialogue between Father Eymard and Christ who is surrendering himself to us in the mystery of the Eucharist. Father Eymard understood that the only response he could give to such a gift was by the gift of himself: "*Gift of myself, this is true love, only this.*" (NR 44,9), " My son, give me your heart." (Pr. 23,26).

In fact, the entire retreat is situated in a context of gift, reciprocity, mutual love. The word "gift," the words "to give" and " to give oneself" return continually and constitute the main theme of his notes.

In his retreat notes, we find several entries which are references to the Word of God in the liturgy, to the celebration of the Mass, to communion and adoration in spirit and in truth. These occasions become the times when Father Eymard would give himself anew to the love of Jesus-Christ, and to renew his [self] gift. (cf. NR 44,78.99). He was living in a continual atmosphere of prayer.

"Sustain me, Lord, by the grace of your Holy Spirit. Strengthen me interiorly by your grace... Give me,

Lord, heavenly wisdom, so that I may learn to seek you and to find you, to enjoy you and to love you above all things, and to count the rest for what it is, according to the order of your wisdom.[…] Behold the whole secret! To give myself to Our Lord unconditionally. I made this gift and took an oath on it before the most Blessed Sacrament at the consecration" (NR 44,42).

During his thanksgiving following the Mass of March 21, 1865, Father Eymard made the vow of his personality as a response to the love of Christ manifested in the Eucharist. He amplified freely a text taken from the *Christian Catechism for the Interior Life* by M. Olier, a representative of the French school of spirituality. He put the text in the first person and placed words on the lips of Christ, as if in a dialogue: " *I will be the person of your personality and your personality will be the life of mine in you.*" (NR 44, 119).

This is how he expressed his desire to consecrate himself to Christ and to draw life totally from him. In this account, he mentioned Communion twice:

"It is thus to abide in me that he gives himself in the Holy Communion. "As the living Father has sent me and I live because of the Father, so he who eats Me, will live because of me" [Jn.6:57]… So, by communion, you will live for Me, for I shall be living in you (NR 44, 119).

The Eucharist is the source for the gift of personality; it is also its model and its means; in fact it communicates the life which the Son has from the Father. The communicant will live for and by Jesus Christ (cf. Jn. 6:57), who will be living in him:

> *"That is what these words of Jesus mean: Whoever eats me, will also live because of me: that is, either by me as his principle, his law, his inspiration, or for me, as his end, in order to please me, to prefer me to everything" (NR 44,80).*

The proper effect of the Eucharist has taken place in Father Eymard by the gift of personality: transformation into Jesus Christ, the transformation of man in God. This is what the saints have affirmed, as did Thomas Aquinas, or the Vatican II Council: "Participation in the body and blood of Christ has no other result than to transform us into what we receive." (LG 26).

The Eucharist makes us one body and one blood with Christ. It is not a physical union that takes place, but a union of our being with the glorified body of Christ present in the Eucharist. We are really one single body, but in a new mystical way. The Eucharist transforms us in Jesus; his faculties, his feelings, his way of thinking, his way of acting become ours.

This life which comes from the Eucharist is none other than the very life of Jesus Christ, which it forms and perfects in us. (PG 319,1). Communion is the life of Jesus Christ in us, Jesus Christ is born, develops, acts in us by communion (PO 12,3).

Father Eymard who had come to Rome for *the important and colossal question* of the Cenacle of Jerusalem, now had to accept the impossibility of bringing it to a happy ending. He realised that God was manifesting his will to him differently and gifting him with greater and more precious interior insights: adoration in spirit and in truth, the soul which becomes the interior cenacle (the "*cenacle in me and the glory of God in me*" (NR 44,23), abiding in love, the life of Jesus Christ in him becoming the "self" of his personality, "*the self of myself" (NR 44,80*). He saw clearly that the kingdom of God begins in us, that the Eucharistic life is to be lived in the depth of the human heart, that conformity to Christ present in the Eucharist consists in being totally united to him: " It is no longer I who live, but Christ who lives in me" (Gal. 2:20).

In mystical terms: by means of the gift of self, Father Eymard received a grace of transformation which renewed him interiorly, he entered deeply into the paschal mystery and shared in the life of the Trinity.

JESUS CHRIST "WANTS TO GLORIFY HIS FATHER IN EACH ONE OF US"

"This vow must be the greatest, the holiest of all the others, since it is the vow of the self, and of a self ever free to give itself anew[...]So then, oh my soul: you will be the members, the faculties of Jesus Christ, in order that he may live and act in all things for the glory of the Father. Our Lord desires this union to better glorify his Father on earth, by incarnating himself in a certain way in each Christian, in order to become like his divine personality[...] It is therefore Our Lord who wants to relive in us, and to continue through us the glorification of his Father[...] By this union then, our actions become the actions of our Lord (NR 44, 120.121).

The vow of personality, the gift of self, became "*the key*" of Father Eymard's whole life. (cf.NR44,10), "*a new path*"(cf. PR 111,2), the characteristic virtue which he proposed to his own. This is the grace of holiness which flows from the Eucharist; " by receiving the Body and Blood of Jesus Christ, we become sharers in the divine life in an ever more mature and conscious way" (SaCa 70).

Father Eymard's passion was to live a life modeled on Christ and united with him. This theme was very present [in the meditations] during the days which followed the vow of personality.

> *"I meditated on our Lord's union with us, a union which must be the life of my vow of personality[...]. Our Lord comes in us sacramentally to live there spiritually (NR 44,121.126)*

Christ was drawing him relentlessly toward this life of union: "*He wants to be my whole life*" (NR 44, 124), said Father Eymard. "*He wants very much to sanctify us in order to unite us to himself and make us live his life*"(NR 44,121). In fact, a spiritual life is the development of the new life of Jesus Christ in us. He meditated on the allegory of the vine and the branches (cf. Jn. 15:1-8), the teaching of St. Paul on the Body of Christ, of which we are members (cf. 1Co. 6:15 and 12:27), and the affirmation of St. Gregory: "the Christian is another Christ."

He understood that the only means to live by this union is:

> *"to nurture and fortify within me the interior man who is Jesus Christ, to conceive him, to bring him forth and make him grow by all my actions, readings, prayers, adorations, and in all the relationships of my life (NR 44, 125).*

We must constantly nurture this union, because union happens by means of union itself. We should resolve to live in union with Christ by desiring it, wanting it; we must abide in Christ (cf. Jn.15:4,5,9). For that, Father Eymard decided to surrender the "*governance*" of his existence, to Christ, and to place himself under his guidance, to "*live in Our Lord, to live by his spirit*" (NR 44,44). By being completely centered on Christ, he found life in him, life, movement and being; Jesus Christ became his counsellor, his strength, his consolation (cf. NR 44,27), his interior master, the guest of his soul and of his body, his guide (cf. NR 44, 127), his model and the God of his heart (cf. NR 44,96).

Filled with the love of Jesus Christ, he wanted to resemble him in all things, have the same sentiments as he did (cf. Ph. 2:5). By living in Jesus Christ, through him, in him and for him, he attained an existential identification:

> *"If I love Jesus, I must resemble him [...] I will be a replica of him, the body of his soul, the freedom of his desires, the human executions which he will make divine by our union" (NR 44,47,60).*

It is the Eucharist "which makes possible, day by day, the progressive transfiguration of all [those] called by grace to reflect the image of the Son of God (cf. Rm. 8:29ff) (SaCa 71). Father Eymard let himself be fashioned by the Eucharist, which was the center of his life:

> *The center which should form and foster the Christian and evangelical virtues, without my having to seek elsewhere; a center which gives me ready nourishment, since it is an atmosphere of light, of sweetness, of peace; indeed it is Our Lord [...] He himself shall live through me because he abides in me" [cf. Jn.6:57-58]. (NR 44,81).*

This union of life occurs through grace and fidelity to it, while also being an adherence to Christ's words, union of faith and love, union with Jesus Christ who makes reference to the unity of life between Jesus and his Father (cf. Jn. 17: 22-23); by analogy it recreates the relationship which exist between Jesus Christ and his Father (cf. Jn. 15:9). This can be seen clearly when Father Eymard quotes the passage of Jn. 14:10: "The Father living in me accomplishes his works", and writes immediately following: "*Christ living in me accomplishes his works"(cf. NR 44,60).*

> *"I must therefore be united to our Lord Jesus Christ as his human nature was to the authority of his divine person, as Jesus was totally to his Father. But in order to be so, one must be united with the union of life received from him and communicated by him. (NR 44,124)."*

Consequently, life as a whole becomes an extension of the life of Christ, "*our actions become the actions of our Lord*" (NR 44, 121). "*This union of the person with Our Lord constitutes his dignity."[...]"By my union with Our Lord I become something sacred, holy"(*NR 44, 122).

By living in this way, Father Eymard was able to find grace, freedom, peace, life, union with God (cf. NR 44,44,63), his life became fullness of life. He found everything in Jesus Christ; he felt at ease, at home, under his guidance.(cf.NR 44,44).

Father Eymard writes: It is "*the Holy Spirit who accepts to form us in this new life*" (NR 44,64). The vow of personality is not the result of willful effort, nor personal achievement, it is a grace, above all it is the fruit of the action of the Holy Spirit. As he sought to understand how to attain this life, he reflected on the angel's words to Mary: "The Holy Spirit will come upon you, and the power of the Most High will overshadow you.." (Lk. 1:35).

The Holy Spirit who brought about the incarnation of Jesus Christ in Mary , who makes Christ present on the altar, effects his presence in the human person by vivifying Christ in him.

There is, in fact, a profound analogy between the action of the Spirit coming upon Mary and the coming of the Spirit on the bread and wine to transform and make them bearers of the life-giving dynamism of the Risen Lord; and there also exists an analogy, more profound yet, between the coming of the Spirit on Mary and his coming in us for our Eucharistic conversion, so that we may become "`the One we have received"(cf. EE 56-57).

By the gift of ourselves, Christ is glorified in us (cf. Jn. 17:10; NR 45,7); we become the true glory which the Father longs for, the new person recreated in Christ (cf.Eph2:15). Father Eymard wrote:

> *"Oh! If we could understand these words of St. Paul: "It is no longer I who live, it is Jesus-Christ living in me" (Gal.2;20); and these: "and form in us that perfect man who is Jesus Christ come to full stature"(cf. Eph. 4:13). Yes, Jesus Christ has a spiritual birth and development in each person. He wants to glorify his Father in each one of us" (CO 1547-1695*).*

During the celebration of the Eucharist, we ask the Holy Spirit to make each of us an eternal offering to the glory of the Father that we may become in Christ a living offering to the praise of his glory, so that together with all creation we may glorify the Father through Christ.

TO KNEAD " THE NEW BREAD" OF MY POOR SOUL

"I admire the good Master's way of forcing me into solitude, and now, I'm very happy about it. Not that I want anything more, no! But I see more clearly. All that remains now is to knead this new bread of my poor soul. I won't give you any today, that would be taken from the old [bread] which you have been familiar with for such a long time and which did not always suit you, because it was too old! We will give you something new when we arrive. In the meantime, let me tell you very simply: [...] Live from our Lord, in our Lord, and for our Lord. "Whoever abides in Me and I in him, says our Lord, that one does great things! "Therefore, dwell in our Lord; but you say to me, how? By putting yourself aside. (Co 1542–1539).*

Father Eymard wrote these words from Rome

about 10 days before making the vow of personality, in a letter to Mother Guyot, the superior of the Religious of Saint Thomas-de-Villeneuve. It was her who had provided his daily bread during the first days of the foundation of the Congregation. And he promised to give her "*some new bread*" on his return. In a letter to Mme Jordan, he invited his correspondent to "*profit from the bread of life* of Jesus Christ, *that is, live with him, within him, rather than within yourself.*" (CO 1541 –1538*).

The theme of bread can also be found in his retreat notes from Rome (1865). On February 1st, he meditated on the words of St. Ignatius of Antioch, martyr: "I am the wheat of Christ" and added: "*May I be ground by mortification, may I be baked by the fire of love, so that I may become pure bread.*" (MR 44,14).

Father Eymard became like "new dough... like Easter bread" (1Co 5:7), he entered into "full communion with the Pasch of Jesus Christ and thus became Eucharist with Him". (SaCa 85). He heard as if addressed to himself the invitation of Jesus Christ to his disciples: "Give them yourselves bread to eat" (Lk. 9:13), he confirmed that "the vocation of each one of us consists in truly "being bread broken for the life of the world with Jesus." (SaCa 88).

It is evident that during the Retreat of Rome, Father Eymard received a grace of transformation which renewed him interiorly; henceforth he would experience the paschal dimension and dynamism of the Eucharist. In the footsteps of Christ Jesus who annihilated himself on the cross, he accepted that same emptying to receive the new life given by the Risen Christ, exalted at the right of the Father, a life transformed by the Holy Spirit.

By this renunciation of his personal will, Father Eymard belonged entirely to God, he lived a life centered on God, a life guided by love and in love. He surrendered himself totally to the will of God and acted uniquely for Jesus Christ. On March 30 1865, the last day of the Great Retreat of Rome, he wrote to Father de Cuers:

> *"Let us adore God's plans and praise his holy will![…] the Sacred Congregation decided to leave the status quo and not to change anything in the previous order of things, that nothing can be done for the moment.[…]I can only say: May your will be done! (CO 1546-1543*).*

Something changed in his relationship with people. During the retreat, he suffered trials, criticisms and misunderstanding even from some of his religious (cf. NR 44, 91). But in the midst of these difficulties, he withheld any judgment of persons, excused them, he chose silence (cf.NR 44,138), patience, "*I saw Our Lord calm and kind in the midst of those who were hurting him so", (NR 44, 91)*, gentleness, *(I repeated: Jesus, meek and humble of heart, make my heart like unto thine." [...] Gentleness should be the characteristic grace of his followers because it is the fruit of love", (NR 44, 91.97)*, charity, service (" *I must be the servant of the servants [of God], the disciple of my Master, meek and humble of heart!" (NR 44,46)*, and prayer, in order to hold back his personal will, nor be overbearing in his position as superior.

> *You must serve Jesus and all the "Jesus" whom he has entrusted to you, with joy and happiness, with the devotedness of Saint Joseph. "Insofar as you have done this to one of my little ones [of my brethren} you have done it to me"[Mt. 25:40] (NR 44,112).*

That is how his new self, his interior self prevailed *"[the self] who is Jesus Christ in me"(NR 44, 125)* who lives by " *the fortitude born of love" (NR 44, 138).*

On returning to France on Saturday April 8, 1865, Father Eymard went to the home of Mrs. Nathalie Jordan, in Lyons. He stayed there until the following Tuesday, sharing his Roman experience with her and her daughter.

A very interesting exchange of letters took place in the days that followed. In response to Mme Jordan who thanked him for his sharing, he wrote on April 22:

"You were given the first fruits of Rome[...]; I was only a poor receptacle which still held the perfume of what it had received, so kindly, from God." (CO 1551- 1547)*

Nathalie's niece, Edmee Brenier de Montmorand, who was living in Shanghai (China), wrote to her aunt in reply to the latter's sharing about her conversation with Father Eymard: " I spent so much time reading and rereading your letter... It is hard to explain, but it is as if I had inhaled a delightful perfume."

Father Eymard's Roman experience of the gift of his personality had become like a perfume, and everyone who met him could enjoy it.

This image of perfume reminds us of the anointing at Bethany (cf. Jn.12:1-8), where a woman poured out a precious perfume in a gesture of gratuitous love. Father Eymard had given himself to Christ, and his humanity was transformed by it; he showed forth the life of Jesus in him, he became "the sweet scent of Christ" (2Cor. 2,15). He wrote: "*to be Christian is to imitate his example, in order to be the sweet scent of Christ, for the Christian is another Christ*" (PG 125,1).

Christ etches a new dynamism into our existence, we become witnesses of his love, and "through our actions, words and way of being, Another makes himself present." (SaCa 85).

One month before his death, Father Eymard invited the Servants of the Blessed Sacrament to give their personality to Jesus-Christ, to strive for perfection and to say with St. Paul; "It is no longer I who live, it is our Lord Jesus Christ who lives in me." (Gal. 2:20). He reassured them:

> *[..] then you will be happy, very fortunate. Your heart will be full, nothing will be holding it back, you will be all-powerful with the power of Our Lord. (PS 642,3).*

It was a sort of testimony. "There is nothing authentically human - our thoughts and affections, our words and deeds - that does not find in the sacrament of the Eucharist the form it needs to be lived to the full" (SaCa 71).

" MY TRINITARIAN FAMILY WHICH I BLESS WHOLEHEARTEDLY"

"Very dear Madame in Our Lord, I greet you from [my passenger] coach, you and your beloved family, sorry that I don't have a day to spare on my way down to go to see you at Calet [...] If I have a day when I return, I will give you half [...] You must be like busy Martha, do try to wed these two dear sisters of Bethany a little more; if Martha's place is more meritorious, Mary's is more delightful [cf.Lk10:38-42]. Your dear nieces must be with you, happy to be with their dear aunt. So I bless my Trinitarian family wholeheartedly [...] Goodbye, dear Lady, don't forget that I am getting older and I am not getting better. I don't know how to belong fully to God in the midst of winds and waves. (CO 1401-1399).*

Father Eymard had a great gift for dialogue with his contemporaries. His vision of the Eucharist deeply stirred the men and women he met; many of them turned to him for advice. His invitation to a life of union with God deeply marked individuals and families, religious men and women and priests as well.

In his ministry as a spiritual director he sought to discern how grace was at work in each person. "*for God speaks to the soul in a thousand ways.*" (cf. PT 124, 4). He would show them the way to God, and help them to find their place in the Church and society.

His vision of the Church corresponded to an image used by St. Augustine:

> *The Church is a garden where each flower has its place, its perfume, its dew, its blessing, where all exists only for the glory of God." (CO 630-631*).*

Two examples will suffice here. Father Eymard received Auguste Rodin as a novice in his community. Auguste was upset following the death of his sister who had been a member of a religious community. Father Eymard allowed him to pursue his work as a sculptor. In May 1863, young Rodin left the community to follow his real vocation as a sculptor. Isabelle Spazzier, a painter, was dreaming of religious life and was part of the very first group of the Servants. Then, following Father Eymard's advice, she returned to her life as an artist:

"Always go to God with the soul of an artist, that is the right word, and it is a charming, very accurate idea. We go to God as he has made us and as we are. Yes, be God's artist, gather everything up and offer it to him. [...] We must go to God on the path he makes available to us in this world" (CO 692- 695).*

From the outset of his foundation, Father Eymard desired to associate priests and laity to his ideal. Undoubtedly, his pastoral experience as director of the Third Order of Mary had made him attentive to their spiritual needs. He was convinced that the Eucharist belongs to the whole Church, that the "Eucharistic grace" is poured out generously and can be lived out in various ways.

He thought of an "aggregation" for the laity and attempted several times to write a "Guidebook for Aggregates" which would offer them a spirituality, a rule of life. Though he did not manage to complete this work, either for lack of time or method, its goal is perceptible nonetheless:

"To form good and fervent adorers in the world for our Lord Jesus Christ in his Sacrament of love, where he is so neglected and offended; to join their efforts together to serve the Eucharist; and to help

them to live more perfectly of the very life of Jesus in the Blessed Sacrament (RA 8,1)."

Father Eymard's goal then was to form the laity to the Eucharistic life as the summit of their Christian life. They would participate in this way in the spirit of the Congregation, be "its spiritual members" and share its purpose and works.

He saw the love of God as the sovereign law of the Christian life, its principle, center and purpose. He contemplated this law in the love of Christ who has given us the Eucharist. He cast light upon the "centrality" of the holy Eucharist in the life of the Church. At the same time, he sought to show the bond between Eucharistic life and community, and invited them to "join their efforts together", that is, to be a community inspired by the Eucharist, living a life of prayer in liturgical worship and the service of adoration; a life of unity, based on the gospel spirit; a life of mission, centered on the Eucharist. We can say that the inspiration for this project stemmed from the Eucharist as communion.

In Father Eymard's correspondence, we find the suggestions he gave to the members of the Aggregation regarding their lives and work. He transmitted to them his apostolic ardour, the fire of Eucharistic love.

"Remain always an apostle of the God of the Eucharist; it is a mission of fire around those who are cold, of light for those who do not believe, of holiness for the soul of the adorer. Jesus has said: "I am the Bread of life" [Jn. 6:35] (CO 1344).

He asked them to turn their homes into "*a little family of adorers*" (CO 2075– 2076*), or a *'Bethany of our Lord, the permanent Cenacle of his Eucharistic life!'* (CO 2075–2076*)

The experience of the Aggregation is a way of Christian formation, of personal and communal maturation in the light of the Eucharist, so that the faithful may become, as Vatican II declared, a catalyst for renewal in the world. (cf. AA 2).

Father Eymard`s activity did not limit itself only to the laity, but he also reached out to priests. His sensitivity to their life situation dated from his own personal experience as vicar at Chatte and as pastor at Monteynard at the beginning of his ministry and then to his friendship with the Curé d'Ars.

Father Eymard felt impelled to dedicate himself to their sanctification, aware as he was of the loneliness from which so many priests suffer, of their spiritual distress and their lack of devotion toward the Eucharist (cf. CO 1099), he wrote:

"I understand more than ever that to rekindle, nourish and perfect the spirit of Eucharistic devotion among priests is the work par excellence, the most necessary of all (CO 698 - 701).*

In his project to restore the Christian life to its own center, the Eucharist, he considered priests as "*multipliers,*" that is, the ones whose actions aim at spreading the kingdom of Jesus Christ; "*in fact, to help a priest,*" he said," *is to help thousands of souls*". He dreamed of creating fraternities to encourage their growth in Eucharistic spirituality, he wanted to "*sanctify priests by the Eucharist*".

We must also say that Father Eymard was greatly enriched by all the people he met during his lifetime. They contributed to his personal growth, his vision of the Eucharist, and were of benefit to his life's project. His experience helped him grow in understanding the Church as a communion, as a pilgrim people of God, where vocations, responsibilities, charisms and ministries are interrelated, each at the service of the others, where each element makes its own contribution to others and to the whole Church (cf. LG 13), and where all together serve the Christian community in its [work] of building the kingdom of God.

"BE LED INTERIORLY BY HIS DIVINE SPIRIT"

"Let yourself be led interiorly by his divine Spirit, and externally by his fatherly Providence in keeping with your grace and total self-giving [...] Nourish yourself on our Lord, on his spirit, his virtues, his evangelical truth, on the contemplation of his mysteries. Do not leave him. He said: "If you abide in me and my words abide in you, everything that you want will be done." [Jn.15:7]. Place yourself, not in the rays, but in the sun, and you will have all the rays in their essence. In everything that you do, discover the bread of life of Jesus, and then nothing will weaken you [...] Dear daughter, study, study our Lord, and try to understand him, to discover his secrets, the motives of his heart, and you shall be thrilled. Always go towards his heart: this source and happiness of life. Give your neighbor the flames of

your devoted heart, but leave this heart in the heart of Jesus, and you will have nothing to lose, nothing to fear. (CO 2171)

Father Eymard addressed to everyone without distinction of social condition, status of life, or age, this invitation to tend toward the interior life and devote themselves to it: everyone must apply themselves to becoming interior in order to live with God, to act in union with God, to be happy in God (cf. CO 1797-Nil*), to be in control of oneself, to recollect oneself *"from external things to those within."*(CO 861)

Dom Paul Marechal, who had known Father Eymard, and would eventually leave the Congregation, would speak about his great zeal for his neighbor and his gifts as an apostle, being at the same time an essentially interior soul living in close and constant union with God.

This testimony can be substantiated by Father Eymard's words to Mme Jordan: *"I envy your gentle rest. I am in the midst of this billowing ocean called Paris, where I take hold of God on the run and rest a little when I adore him."* (CO 1380-1379*)

The invitation to the interior life finds its inspiration in the words of Jesus at the Last Supper (cf. Jn. 13-17), where the verb "abide' is used in different grammatical declensions.

We abide in Jesus Christ when we love his will and contemplate his goodness and providence (cf. CO 1182-1181*), believing in the love of God in every situation, because "*the nature of the sun does not change because the passing clouds veil it (*CO 2075-2076*).

We abide in Jesus-Christ when we let ourselves be led by the Holy Spirit, let him speak and act in us. The Holy Spirit forms Jesus in us, so that we may live by his divine and risen life (cf. RA 18,11). He is our educator and sanctifier, he teaches us the truth about Jesus and gives us the strength to be his faithful and generous witnesses; he prays and groans in us with ineffable groanings of love (cf. Rm. 8:26). His action completes that of the Father and of the Son.

> *"St. Paul calls our body the temple of the Holy Spirit [1Co6:19], therefore he abides in us– Jesus Christ has given him to us so that he may always be with us [Jn.14:16]. The Holy Spirit: See that the Kingdom of God is in your midst [Lk.17:21].– All the glory and beauty of the King's daughter is within [Ps 44:14] (NR 44, 126).*

We must therefore let the holy Spirit work in us and be docile in his hands " *like soft wax which receives his imprint*" in a word, [let him] continue Pentecost in us (cf. PP 31,1).

To abide means to live in close intimacy with God, in a "*love of friendship*". This love of friendship:

> "..*is the life of every soul which lives not just for Jesus, but by Jesus, by his intimate life, and which recognizes his hidden action in all things, which sees the sign of his love in all things (NR 44, 85).*

God speaks the language of the heart *"which only love can hear and understand"* (CO 861-0861*). Whoever attains the interior life loves God and enters into the very essence of love: *The human person is love, just as God is love .To love God truly, we must love from within" (PS 283,1).*

This intimate life with God fills the person with joy, its loss`provokes great desolation, comparable to the desert and to an agony.

The last years of Father Eymard's life were marked by such a desert: spiritual dryness, the dimming of faith, total numbness, vain calls to God who seemed deaf to his cries. In this difficult context, he made a personal retreat (from April 27 to May 2, 1868), which can be considered as "his spiritual testament".

His notes seem to unveil a few aspects of this silence of God, which is comparable to a spiritual night.

I prayed ardently for the resurrection of this grace; the state of my soul, now for three years so distressed, so sad, so desolate. [...] My soul is ice cold. Jesus no longer lets his sun shine.[...] The depths of my heart is waiting for God [...] My soul[...] suffers from Our Lord's silence. This prolonged silence leaves me desolate. (NR 45,3.11.14).

The retreat began with thanksgiving: God is and ever remains the God of love. God began to speak to him anew, to reveal himself, to manifest himself. God granted him a "*merciful hearing*", gave him the grace of prayer, the proof of his love, treating him " *as a bosom friend*" (cf. NR 45,1*)*. It is like a resurrection song!

This experience of God's friendship reminds us somewhat of the affirmation of Vatican II: "God, who is invisible, addresses himself to mankind as friends, and speaks with them to invite them to enter into fellowship with him and to receive them into this communion." (DV 2).

God manifests his love by addressing himself to mankind; his word creates a covenant, friendship and communion. This friendship between God and men finds its summit in Jesus-Christ; at the Last Supper, he called his disciples, "friends" , "because everything that I have heard from my Father, I have made known to you" (Jn.15:15).

So the painful time experienced by Father Eymard became a grace and an impulse toward a new beginning. The meditations found at the end of this retreat enable us to perceive the direction of life he took just a few months before his death. He was hoping for a prayer of repose, "a living prayer".

Oh! How I needed now this prayer of repose at the feet of the Master. "Come aside in a deserted place and rest a while"[Mk. 6:31]. – a repose at the feet of Jesus, a rest that craves for his grace, his goodness, his mercy, - one look of love from Him, a quiet and peace for my whole being,- a loving and refreshing repose. I enjoyed a brief moment of that repose. How I long for that other prayer the Savior speaks of! 'I will bring her into the wilderness and I will speak tenderly to her heart." [Hos. 2:16] (NR 45,14).

That desert to which Father Eymard felt invited was the place of God's Covenant with his people; his ardent search for God evoked that of the spouse of the Canticle of Canticles. *"I am God's daytime worker"* (NR 45,16), he wrote. From this point on, he was ready for an ever more complete gift of himself, and he offered God the three *flowers: humility, purity, fidelity"* (NR 45,16).

"MAN HUNGERS FOR GOD"

"Man hungers for God and Jesus Christ is their only divine food. Until they eat the living bread who has come down from heaven, they will be hungry; until they drink from this chalice of salvation, they will thirst. We must then give this divine viaticum to these poor travelers lest they faint."(RA 16,7).

When Father Eymard arrived in Paris on April 30, 1856, he was coming to a city which was in the midst of total transformation: by the end of the century the population would multiply fourfold. Industrial development created a large, poverty-stricken, working class under the duress of difficult working conditions, unhealthy living situations, and deprived of any rights. (Corporations had been suppressed during the Revolution and unions were forbidden.)

Father Eymard was aware that manufacturers viewed people solely as work engines, and like the majority of the church-people of his times he considered charity and religious education as the means to remedy social problems. What distressed him, was to see part of the population becoming de-Christianised: "*It is frightening to see so many men who have not made their first communion*"(CO 609-0611*). In an effort to respond to this situation, he endeavored to establish the Work for the First Communion of young workers.

His first efforts were not very successful as it was it impossible to organise this apostolate due to the community's unstable situation. He was able to dedicate himself to it only three years after the foundation, when the community settled at Faubourg St. Jacques. He began by searching for the young workers, waiting for them at the factory gates; he went among the rag-pickers in the poor neighborhoods, he surveyed the 'territory'. With the collaboration of the laity, he succeeded in gathering an initial group of young men who would make their first Communion on August 15, 1859. We can say that the work was in progress by Christmas of that same year.

Three celebrations a year for groups of 30 or 40 communicants became the norm. The meetings were held in the evenings three times a week, after the day's work. Father Eymard developed a pedagogy to arouse interest and participation. After his first communion, each participant was to find a replacement; the young men thus became apostles in their own environment and in their families.

Each celebration was preceded by a three day retreat. This prepared the young men for their admission to make their profession of faith, to receive Eucharistic communion and Confirmation; several of them were even prepared for baptism.

In fact, Father Eymard's pastoral work was a true catechumenate for adolescents and young workers. By means of first communion he desired to open them to the transforming love of Christ in the Eucharist. He worked to bring about " the rebirth' of Jesus Christ in his children. He wrote to one of his collaborators:

> *"Today we had a great feast! The first communion of 18 children, some of whom were from 16–18 years of age. They really edified and consoled us; what a change takes place in them! These wild, rude, brutish types when they arrive, these little street urchins gradually become more humane. They become attentive, grateful, good and virtuous. First communion changes them completely. They are no longer the same! Their hearts are open and there, we find generous and gentle sentiments." (CO 908-907*).*

From August 15 to June 28 1868, the final celebration in which Father Eymard participated, 24 ceremonies had associated 766 young boys according to the register (the feminine branch, the Servants of the Blessed Sacrament, worked for the young women as well, during their presence in Paris).

By working thus for the first communion of adults, Father Eymard established a connection between worship of the Eucharist, catechesis and missionary action. Starting from this experience, his ambition was to encircle the city of Paris with centers of catechesis; he was envisioning 4 to 8 centers.

He did not limit his help to the young workers only during the preparatory period for their first Communion. Father Eymard was careful to integrate them into the Christian community; he would gather them periodically, invite them to strengthen their faith, evaluate their Christian commitment, prepare them for their Easter duties; most of them would come: "*They know that they are known and loved*" (RA 31,5). His concern was to build relationships and a warm family atmosphere.

The inspiration for Father Eymard's commitment to the workers in the outskirts of Paris sprang from the Eucharist and the Word of God. In a letter he once referred to it as " *the beautiful and lovely mission; the royal mission of the Eucharistic wedding feast* " (CO

1099). He was convinced of the deep bond between Christ's presence in the Eucharist and Christ's presence in his brothers and sisters, particularly in society's poor and marginalised people. Two passages of the Gospel inspired him greatly: the parable of those invited to the banquet (cf. Lk. 14:15-24) and the passage on the judgment of the nations (cf. Mt. 25:31-46).

He saw "*the Eucharist as the wedding feast of the Son of the great king*" (PS 14,1) "*The wedding feast of each Christian with Jesus Christ. [...] There is no greater honor than that.* (PS 19,15). He wanted the poor to rediscover their dignity, to enhance the sense of worth of these young people who were scorned by the world, give meaning to their lives; he considered it an honor to dedicate himself to this mission: "*We consider them as 12 kings, they represent |Jesus Christ.*" (PS 170,1). He wrote the following to a woman who was caring for the financial aspect of the project in order to clothe the first communicants and compensate for their loss of salary on their retreat days:

> *"As for the money, the One who will send us knows very well that we must dress and help these little children of his grace [...] How pleased our Lord will be with you! Then he will surely say with truth and love: You clothed me in my communicants, you gave me spiritual bread and a bit of material bread! I say*

material bread, Madame, for when these poor little workers are out of work, they come to us whom they call their Fathers. (CO 1742 –CO 1744).*

Father Eymard was convinced that people are hungry for God, that Jesus is their only food, and that our mission is to respond to their hunger. In the Eucharist, Jesus is present with all his love for all people. Christ, in the Eucharist, opens us to universal brotherhood; he teaches us how all people are really equal, all children of God, all candidates to form his body, without any favoritism nor discrimination. It is around the Eucharistic mystery that is born "the service of charity toward one's neighbor" (SaCa 88).

He loves all his children equally. He wants to give himself equally to all, therefore we must continue the Eucharistic supper, keep the door of the King's banquet always open to everyone. (PG 294,6).

These words were [spoken]regarding the work of the First Communion of adults; but today this text assumes new shades of meaning. We receive these words with great humility in the presence of the new challenges which face the Church today so that all may enter into the banquet hall and feel that they are welcomed. The Eucharist urges us to work for unity, to be attentive to the cry of the poor and to collaborate with other leaders so that the dignity of every man be recognized and respected. (cf. SaCa 89)

"MARY'S GREAT MISSION IS TO FORM JESUS IN US"

"Be fervent daughters of Mary, the Queen and Mother of the Servants of God. On the cross Jesus was telling you personally: Daughter, here is your Mother [cf.Jn.19:27].This claim which Jesus gave you over his Mother's heart was not in vain , rather this last wish of our Savior entitles you to take his place there [....]Therefore my sisters, let Mary's spirit be an inspiration for you. Her spirit was the same as that of Jesus[...] She is the only true and perfect copy of Jesus' virtues.[...]Mary's great mission is to form Jesus in us[...] Honor all the divine mysteries of her life as so many steps to the Cenacle. Let Mary's life in the Cenacle be the model and consolation of your life. Honor this life of Mary in the Eucharistic Cenacle, it is your beautiful heritage, my sisters (RS 12,55)."

Father Eymard's Marian devotion took root in his childhood. It developed during his pilgrimages and visits to sanctuaries dedicated to Mary. These would become so many landmarks along his [life] journey.

At 11 years of age, to prepare for his first communion, he set out for the shrine of Notre–Dame du Laus, which is about 80 kilometers from La Mure. This shrine, which he called a "*touching and attractive pilgrimage of grace and love,*" was the place of his vocational call, as he wrote in a letter: *For it is there that I received my vocation from the hands of the Blessed Virgin*"(CO 27-CO 28*).

The priest whom he met at Laus, Father Touche, authorized him to receive communion every Sunday, confirmed his attraction for the priesthood and urged him to study Latin, that is, not to let his father's refusal stand in the way as he sought to answer God's call. This is where he experienced Mary's motherliness in a particular way: "*There, Mary is so motherly, so kind, so tender!*" (CO 260-261*)

On August 5, 1828, upon learning about the death of his mother, Madeleine Pelorce, Father Eymard chose the Virgin Mary to be his mother. He would later note:

"I meditated on the Blessed Virgin's love for me since

my childhood. I thanked our Lady of Laus and the day I took her for my mother when my dear mother died ! Since then, so many graces! At her feet in the chapel of Saint-Robert, I prayed that I might one day become a priest !" (NR 44,109.)

Father Eymard discerned the presence of the Virgin Mary in every stage which lead him to his vocation as a founder. He attributed his priestly vocation to her and especially:

"The grace of the most Blessed Sacrament. She [Mary] gave me to her Son as his servant, his tender child [...] She alone led me by the hand to the priesthood! And then to the Blessed Sacrament! (NR 44,94,109.)"

In 1837 he returned to Laus as a young priest for a retreat a few weeks before his assignment as pastor at Monteynard. In 1839, he fulfilled his heart's profound desire when he entered the Marists, to be part of a society honored with the name of Mary. From that time onward he began to learn the Marist spirituality.

He sent to the altar of the basilica of Laus his project for the Institute which he was preparing to establish so that it would be *"a bouquet of love for this good Mother"* (CO 502-506*).

Having gone through so many separations and stages in his life (as a priest, as a Marist religious, and as a founder), Father Eymard perceived the continuity and special presence of Mary: his consecration to Mary led him to consecrate himself to the Eucharist.

After the foundation of the Congregation, Father Eymard contemplated Mary, no longer only at Nazareth (following the Marist spirituality), but in the Cenacle, at the heart of the first community gathered after the Ascension in expectation of Pentecost (cf. Ac 1:14), assiduous to the breaking of bread and living by the Eucharist (cf. Ac.2:42).

"From Nazareth, Jesus went to the Cenacle and that is where Mary made her final dwelling" (CO 477-481*), he wrote to Marguerite Guillot, who would be the first Servant of the Blessed Sacrament. He invited her to join him in his project, to "*come from Nazareth to the Cenacle*" and to honor Mary, Mother and Queen of the Eucharistic Cenacle (cf. CO 630 – 631*), "*to form real adorers of Jesus Eucharistic, modeled after Our Lady in the Cenacle, adoring and living near the divine Tabernacle*" *(624-625*).*

Even after the foundation, he continued to attribute to the Virgin Mary all the favors which he received himself or that were received by the Congregation:

"Ánd so many graces since 1856: grace of perseverance [...] grace of unity in spite of influences to the contrary [...] then all the graces granted to the Society itself! (NR 44,94.)

Father Eymard imagined Mary spending the last years of her life in the Cenacle in a permanent prayer of adoration for the new-born Church. He proposed to his congregations that they should imitate her as *"a perfect adorer, dedicated to the salvation of the world"*, to share her love for Jesus Christ and her dedication to his glory (cf. RR 78,24 and RS 14,36). He insisted on this life in the Cenacle, characterized by recollection, simplicity of life and prayer centered on the Eucharist and at the service of the Church.

Father Eymard saw the link between the image of Mary praying in the Cenacle and the image of Mary *"the first adorer of the Incarnate Word"*. He wanted to adore Jesus –Christ in union with the Virgin Mary, "*the Mother of adorers and Queen of the Cenacle*", and to share in her spirit: humility for having been chosen as mother of God; joyful gratitude, joined with love, praise and blessing for the goodness of God toward humanity; self-offering and total availability: " Behold the handmaid of the Lord" (Lk. 1:38); and finally, her compassion and mercy for sinners and her intercession to obtain their forgiveness and to ask for their return to God (cf. NR 44, 130).

In his encyclical *Ecclesia de Eucharistia,* Pope John Paul II said that in the mystery of the Incarnation, Mary had anticipated the Eucharistic faith of the Church, she, the first "tabernacle" of history (cf. EE 55). In the school of Mary, he invites us to be conformed to Christ by allowing ourselves by accompanied by her, the "Eucharistic woman". (cf. EE 57).

This conviction was also Father Eymard's, that Mary's great mission was to *"form Jesus in us";* that would require that we imitate her life, especially her interior spirit.

> *"She thought the thoughts of Jesus [...] She busied herself interiorly only with Jesus or for Jesus or in Jesus. And then she was so gentle, so humble, so much at the service of all! [...] Hers was the charity of her divine Son. I prayed to this good Mother for the spirit of meekness, her sweetness, her calm, her patient prudence and wisdom (NR 44,94)."*

On May 1st 1868, Father Eymard suggested that his members honor the Virgin Mary under the title of Our Lady of the Most Blessed Sacrament, emphasizing the important connection of these two words: "Mary and the Eucharist" as well as their connection with the Church. " If Church and Eucharist are inseparable," John Paul II would write again, "we must say as much about Mary and the Eucharist" (EE 57).

"THY KINGDOM COME"

"Our century is ill because it does not adore! It is only through the Eucharist that Jesus-Christ shall reign once again. Be ardent adorers of the holy Eucharist, but in your devotions [you should] especially avoid partisanship: there is only one baptism, one priesthood, one God! Jesus died on the mountaintop in full view of all, to teach us that God's [work] prevails over everything. What kind of catholic would say: "I go only to my parish"? A catholic heart must be as wide as God's! So avoid narrowness in your piety, narrow virtue which shrinks the soul; on the contrary, devotion is like a life-giving sun which expands the heart as it sets it ablaze! Be magnanimous in your view of things, broad in your desires, great in your love! (PO 20,30)."

Father Seymat wrote in a testimony soon after Father Eymard's death that Eymard had found the right expression to state his ideal with the acronym: "A.R.T." ("Adveniat Regnum Tuum", "May Your Kingdom come"). He would then use it as a heading on many of this letters.

The coming of the kingdom of Jesus Christ was Father Eymard's passion, a goal he was constantly striving for: " *I would so love to bring about the kingdom of Jesus Christ on earth!* (CO 479-483*), he wrote. "*May your kingdom come*", was his constant prayer (cf.CO 1486-1481*).

> *"May the Eucharistic kingdom of our Lord come and may we be its first disciples and fervent apostles. No more individualistic pursuits, no more efforts wasted outside [the scope] of our great mission." (CO 1336)*

Obviously, he saw this kingdom as closely linked to the Eucharist, which is " *the kingdom of Jesus Christ in the world, especially in the hearts of his children*"(PR 149,11). To bring about this kingdom, he wished for the gift of one's whole being to Christ (cf. CO 1334). By means of the Eucharist, Jesus Christ "*reigns over individuals and over society (RA 26,5).*

In fact, the Eucharist does give us the perspective of God's kingdom; it is the effective sign of his presence; it lets us enter into it and brings it about. The perspective of the kingdom launches our history toward the future, toward the new [deeds] of God.

Father Eymard wants to give our Lord Jesus Christ:

> *"true and perpetual adorers and to form generous apostles for his glory, zealous communicators of his love, so that the Lord Jesus may always be adored in this Sacrament and glorified socially in the whole world (RR 82t,4).*

For him, the Eucharist was life-giving not only for individuals, but also for the life of society, it has a social dimension. It contains a dynamism of love and unity, its purpose it to have us become "one single body"(cf. 1Cor. 10:16-17). This is how Father Eymard brought the transforming work of the Eucharist to light. As a sacrament of unity it carries with it challenges of reconciliation, justice, sharing and unity. It was after the institution of the Eucharist that Jesus gave us the new commandment and prayed for unity among his disciples. He wrote:

> *"The Eucharist is the bond of fellowship among nations; only family members come to the sacred banquet, at the foot of the altar; there is but one family" (RA 19,7).*

The Eucharist is the bond among Christians, it builds fellowship. Jesus has come to make all people into one single family. "*The Eucharist is the shared bread, and bond of unity between all the children*"(PP36,1);

it destroys jealousy and distinctions, all share at the same table and drink from the same cup; all have the same Father in heaven. A single spirit of charity unites all who eat the same Eucharistic bread. "*Jesus-Christ is then All in all*"(PG 242,3), and the Eucharist is "*the joyful feast of true fellowship, which we can extend forever*"(PG 244,7).

These words of Father Eymard already reverberate with the words of Vatican II: "Christian communities cannot be built up without finding their roots and center in the celebration of the Eucharist (Cf. 2Cor. 12:15): it is therefore the starting point of any formation to a community spirit." (PrOr 6).

Father Eymard was looking at the social situation of his times: the lack of reference points, the disappearance of former guidelines and the rise of individualism following the shock of the revolution. He then proposed the Eucharistic worship as a means of re-centering, of awakening faith, of making Jesus Christ known, and of discovering the love of God.

> *"Society will be reborn vibrant and strong when all its members come to gather around our Emmanuel. Relationships will be rebuilt naturally by this shared truth; the bonds of true and strong friendship will be renewed under the influence of this same love; the beautiful days of the Cenacle, the family Corpus*

Christi, the feast of the great King will be restored" (PG 241,4).

This intuition of Father Eymard is proposed to the Church of our times, now confronted by secularization and the diversity of cultures, and committed to a new evangelization, as the "*path of love*", as the "*most effective means*" to lead our contemporaries to encounter Christ.

"We must bring people to love him. It is by divine love that we must lead the people back to a virtuous life, to religion, to faith. There is no more effective way; it is perhaps even the only way left to us to combat the indifference which reigns in the world and which has even taken over the hearts of the faithful"(PR 149,11).

Father Eymard was aware that God had entrusted him with a mission for the whole world (cf. NR 44, 79). He told his religious: *You are called to set fire to the four corners of the world"*(PR 107,3). Consequently, he invited the adorers to set aside their individuality, their petty selves, in order to bring the world and the universe to the presence of God, especially during their time of prayer:

"Represent classes of peoples, nations, and the universe; do not be there as an individual." (PD 32,8).

Father Eymard often spoke of the Cenacle as a symbolic place which recalls he first Christian community, who were but " one heart and one soul" and shared their possessions (cf. Act. 4:32). But the Cenacle also represents the source of the apostolate of the nascent Church. From the Cenacle, the fearful Apostles who had been closed in on themselves, went out with new courage to convert the world. From that time onward, the *"fire of the first Pentecost, could no longer be extinguished. It gave the apostles the strength of their mission"*(PO 4,9), and the Eucharist is *the continuation of Pentecost, in the Cenacle, with tongues of fire [cf. Act. 2:3]"* (PG 283,2).

For him, the earth itself was like a vast cenacle, and wherever we might be on the planet, we are within this cenacle (PS 401,3).

The Eucharist unites the human community into a single mystery of communion and is able to bring God to the world and the world to God, thanks to its dimension of gratuitous gift. It reveals the social, cultural and political implications of the Gospel to us: it " powerfully illumines human history and the whole cosmos." (SaCa 92).

TABLE OF CONTENTS